I killed myself for a better me

BY
VIJAY KUMAR NAIR

BlueRose ONE.com
Stories Matter

First Published in June 2023

ISBN: 978-93-5819-076-2

BLUEROSE PUBLISHERS

www.BlueRoseONE.com

info@bluerosepublishers.com

+91 8882 898 898

Cover Design:

Vijay Kumar Nair

Typographic Design:

Rohit

Distributed by: BlueRose, Amazon, Flipkart

About my thought of writing the book

It's my dream to publish a book for a long time to write down my thoughts and ideas in my mind. From a long time I'm jotting my thoughts in my mind. After a long struggle with myself, I am starting this book. I Pulled my shocks and started to write this book and try to complete within my set deadline.

Even if this book goes on scrap, I don't care. I will never regret in my life that I could have written a book before I die. After my death, there will be some signature of mine which will exist in this world as an e book or as a hard copy book and in the millions of people around the world, I believe someone from some part of this beautiful world will pick this book and read my thoughts and turn the page to see the Authors name and will find my beautiful Name and I think the person will be little benefited by this book, as I have tried to put down each and everything which I experienced, which I observed, which I felt, which I studied which I heard and overheard and which I read. To the best of my knowledge these are true to a greater extend. Try to include more stories in the book so that along with us our kid within us too can be benefited. After all, the kids within us makes our world colourful.

When I expressed my interest in writing a book to my friends, some of my friends make fun of me and told me. There are millions of books published by highly recognized and world class authors and you think you can manage to find a place in the book shelf along with those big shots. I told them, before and after Sachin Tendulkar there were many world class batsmen, but still Sachin is the God of Cricket.

My dear friends it is not my superior ego. This is the attitude. I don't have name or fame or any ancestral legacy to be proud of or my father is not a rich business tycoon who made me a spoiled kid and more than that I am not born with a silver spoon in mouth. What I have is the attitude which I am trying to build after falling countless times. No one can take it so easily from me. I am not a professional writer and I don't have any experience in writing books. Don't know how to begin a book or how to end it. I even don't take any effort for it. Reason is simple, I feel all the words which I am putting in this should come within me without any limitations or boundaries. No filter or conditions should be applied to it. So my apology at the starting, if I have broken any rules of writing a book.

It's a baby step for me. I may fall and end up with injury or bombarded with negative comments. But one thing is for sure. It won't affect me, now I am trying to understand my value and I don't want get upset by negative annotations and I am in the process to explore the positive side of me with in me. All comments and words, I will definitely consider it as an area to improve myself.

Content of the book

This book is not about some theories regarding motivation or inspirations. That you might have read from many popular authors and might have seen many movies and videos to inspire yourself. But have you ever noticed that in spite of having all these books and videos around us, still now why we are we searching for new motivational tips and techniques. It's easy to give advice. you will find tons of people who are ready to give you free advice. Of course there are genuine personalities too, whom we all admire. But generally you will find everyone around you as an advisor at some or the other level. I think in our country everyone is interested to give free advice, not because that he or she wants to see you grow in your life. Just because they are fed up of the advice that they get from different people. It's like, if I am suffering I will make sure that you also get the share of it. If you don't listen to them, they will curse you. " This boy will do nothing in his life, he is an utter waste as he don't have any respect to elders". Unless and until, if we can relate these advice or motivational comments to our day to day life then only it will make some sense.

From our childhood days we used to listen. Study hard and get good grade, so that you will get respect in the society or will get a decent job or get a beautiful wife with lots of money and if you don't study then your life is like a turmoil and it would like a dark tunnel which has a way to enter but doesn't have an exit. We know all these and we understand the importance of the getting good grades too. Still how many of us got good grades.

The real inspiration or motivation you will get when you don't have a job and every one make fun of you or laugh at you or humiliate you in public. Then you will get the inspiration or motivation to show all those people who humiliated you or laugh at you, which all these books can never can give. Humiliation is the biggest inspiration or motivation factor. I believe, there is no strongest factor than humiliation which can influence you to the extent that you will try every possible thing or to go to any extend to change yourself and put energy from all possible sources in a single point to achieve the goal.

As I mentioned, this book doesn't contain any secret formula or advise as such. I tried to explain each point which I feel it's necessary for you to improve yourself to the next level with some examples from real life and some are imaginary stories. Again If you are turning pages in this book, hoping to get any motivational enlightenment then you are knocking at the wrong door.

Contents

This is not a suicide Note

Please don't take this as my suicide note as said in the title of the book says. Suicide note are written when you lose all your hope and dreams and when you see pitch darkness in front of you. Suicide note is written when the end is dark and this note or the entire book is written where the start is dark but there is a ray of light and hope ahead in the end of tunnel which I am traveling for a long time and I can see the dreams and the colourful world on the other side of the tunnel. Now I see the darkness as darkness of a womb not as the darkness of a tomb. My belief that a new me is about to born soon and the feeling gives me the infinite energy to fight with all adverse situation. I don't want to be a spectator sitting in the gallery and dreaming of playing the game for my entire life. Now its my turn to turn the ball in the ground. Every great things happen in this world is with a small belief. Believe in yourself. Even if you know you are not competent when compared to others, but it's a matter of time. Now it's your time and I respect it and tomorrow will be my time and the world will respect it. Today I don't have any tension, fear or carrying a burden of reputation or image on my shoulder while writing this book. As of now I don't have anything to lose but an entire world to capture. As I don't have any big name and no one is expecting anything extra ordinary creation from me. I don't have to live to up to anyone's expectations and I don't have any fan following or I don't have any subscribers or any readers. So I have the liberty to write anything without any filters and censors. What comes to my mind will directly flow to the paper.

It's a small step for today. But todays baby steps ends up in big milestones tomorrow. It's not an isolated story of me which I am going to tell. More than half of the population in this beautiful world have the same issue. So don't sit and relax by thinking that someone somewhere is killing himself and what I have to do with it. We always forget that we all are connected by some or the other ways. When you are reading this book without you realizing you are connected to me. You don't know me but somehow we started developing a connection and relation. Hopefully it will give sweet and positive results for you and me in future.

Thought of killing the current me

It's been a very long time I am planning to kill the current me. But many of my enemies and not so well wishers of mine were stopping me from executing this act. The nature and all it's forces and my mind always stopped me from executing the act. Daily I try to do it, but I fail always. Now it's been years and still trying.

Every morning, I wake up and think today is the perfect day to execute it .But for no reason instead of killing the current me I started killing time and make the Good Morning to a Good Afternoon and the afternoon I take a nice, peaceful sleep and make it a Good Evening and within few hours, it's dinner time. Have dinner and then go to bed. In between to prove myself that I am good at something, I will try to do something. Which again ends up in wasting my time or doesn't have much value.

Before going to bed, I promise myself. Bro... enough is enough, Tomorrow is your day and I will make no excuse and no one can stop me from killing myself. Then I tried to convince my mind that I am awesome and a unique creation of god and I can do anything in this world. I am much stronger than Thor but the hammer is missing. Tomorrow's sun will see a different version of me. When I feel that my mind is convinced then go for a good sound sleep and next day also it's the same story at the end of day. Same excuse I am stronger and have high will power but the hammer is missing today also . Again to convince my mind, I will make silly excuses and blame everyone except me. Sometimes I feel, it's a conspiracy which is happening against me and I am a victim of this big conspiracy. In front of me days passed and it became months and months passed to become year and years passed and slowly reaching decade. After Kapil Dev and team now MS Dhoni and his team had won the cricket world cup after 28 years but my planning in the morning and excuses in the night continue to be the same and I am sure a couple of decades will pass like this and I will be the same. No goals, no dreams, no passion, no enthusiasm and you can add all the positive words with no in front of it and I clearly relate that it's targeted to me. Still searching for the spark or the starting point when my life is nearing to it's finishing point. Still it's hard to accept the fact that the I am the culprit of my destiny and still blaming others without any shame or regrets.

Now I decided. Today is the day. If the starting point is not coming to me then I have to take efforts and find it anyhow and at any cost. Situation has reached to the edge of patience. Now it's Do Or Die and at last I gathered some courage and strength to perform the act. It would be most challenging task for me and I don't know if I could be able to do it or not. But one thing I know and I am sure that I will put my heart and soul to it and kill the current me once and for all who is killing me every day and every hour. It will take a good decent time to accomplish my mission as my current me has spread its root so deep in me and it's a mammoth task to identify its roots and remove or cut it one by one. It's a painful and challenging task and on each step I have to fight with myself and I don't know how brutal the battle would be. It's like a possessed human fighting with himself to get back his own identity.

Stagnant life

If we summarize our each days activities or we take a short video of each day of our life. We might notice that our each day is very much repetitive and if we delete one or more years of videos, we won't be able to identify it for sure. It's like a clock which will show different time all time but the three needles inside the clock is performing same tasks again and again till its entire their life. Even if its six or eleven the needles task is the same. Its same with us too. My day one will be same as my day two and it's the same as day hundred or day thousand. Can't see any change as we are living the same life day after day, month after month and year after year. Living a life for the sake of living is not a big deal. A stagnant life where there is no difference between start point and end point. If we put our every day to a picture and after two or three years when we compare all the picture you can see it's the same photocopy which has been repeated days and years. Not much change can be noticed. It's very much true that we are social animals. Animals roam in the jungle for food and by evening they will come back home and feed the little once. We also do the same. Only difference is, we go to find food on a more polished way. By wearing tie or by wearing expensive causals in our own vehicle or in Uber or in Metro etc. But the crux is the same. Both man and animal are fighting in jungle or in modern jungle for food. Just one difference. Animals will be happy if there stomach is full. After a full meal tiger wont hunt any pray if the pray comes to its radar also but humans won't be satisfied with full stomach. His demand will switch from one to another.

It's a circle we have trapped in and the circle is so strong it's difficult to get out of it but it's not impossible. Living a stagnant life with all dreams, visions and hopes are compromised for silly confront zones or to some silly excuses. It's like the a soldier who have all the arms and ammunition which hold the power to change the face of the war but the soldier don't want to fight with the arms and ammunition. To give away a battle worth for fight without fighting. It's like owning a 1000 CC Bike and using it to just buy vegetable and fruits from market and we thinks we are using the full potential of the bike. But after a very long year of owning the bike, we don't know the actual potential of bike. Same are we. by having a brain of a 1000 giga bite memory and using it just remember ATM Pin, Gpay pin or mobile pin or pattern.

A life of a looser who always run away from confronting problems and fear of chasing dreams and scared of proving himself to the world . Considering all the opportunity as a complex and cumbersome task and have an excellent analytical brain to identifying all the possible faults, flaws and obstacles for not taking the opportunity. For being a hard core pessimist, who is very good at finding thousand reasons for not doing a task and can't figure out a single reason for doing it.

My Current Me

My mind knows how much I love my comfort zone. To keep me in the comfort zone, it will do all possible tricks in the universe. In the morning when Alarm rang, I wanted to wake up for the Gym, but my mind would say to me. "Look at the bed, it's so pretty and cosy and you want to leave her alone. Come on sleep for some more time". I will say... "No I want to wake up". It will again says. "Okay, we will make a deal. You sleep for 10 min and go wherever you want to go and I start thinking it's a fair deal. Win Win situation for both of us. That 10 Min sleep will end after 3 hours. Then I wake up frustrated cursing myself, my alarm clock and all the possible persons I can see around me. In short, my day starts with frustration and the same mood will continue for the rest of the day.

Next day also repeat the same episode and guess who wins, no prize for guessing. I surrender to my mind without giving a shot. After some days, I quit the plan to go to the gym. It's not only about gym. It's for each and everything. It's a big conspiracy happening within me which I am not aware. When the challenger quit's without challenging then it's a easy game for the opponent. In short on morning itself my game is over.

In office too, I know what I should be doing to climb up the ladder, that extra effort I know where to put and how to put. But the golden words when my mind says to me. Bro. today you sit and relax and enjoy the day. Tomorrow we can start building the career. Enjoy your time today. I fell again in the same trap. On weekends when trying to do something different or at least planning to do something, this man pops out of my brain and tells me, Today is weekend. Are you mad or what. Working on weekends. No need to work. Take rest.

I say. Hai.. I want to-spend some quality time with my wife and kids. Then my mind will say. You sleep now. Where are they going. They are here only. Let them come to you .don't go to them. See you are choosing a difficult path. You have to wake up from bed then you have to go to your kids and you have to play with them under the sun. ehh. You better relax and enjoy the sleep, by the time you wake up. they will come to you. but the reality is, by the time I make up my mind to play and spend time with my kids and wife the weekend would be over. Just like every other weekend I thought the same thoughts and tried to contemplate my decisions. I couldn't battle him and he couldn't leave me.

A small Start to find the Starting Point

Enough is enough, I want to kill the looser or the pessimist in me with whom I have lived for many years. I want to destroy all the filters in my mind who filter all the voices, instructions, messages and gives me only the negative or the information which I barely needed. All the useful information and the instructions to get out of comfort zone or to chase the dreams and follow the passions are filtered and deleted even before it hit my unconscious mind. Today I want to identify all the traitors or enemies who lives inside me but works against me. I think all these entities inside me might be the happiest souls in the planet because from my childhood days onwards they are winning all the battles against me and on every day , every hour , every minute I am losing the battle against them.

What an irony , my mind who I trusted the most and thought that it will make fare and judgemental decisions for me and motivate me to achieve my goals turned to be that coach who gives priority only to his personal need then the teams. My mind is the most biased entity that I have ever met up with. Always thought of its comfort zone and find its ways to stop me from doing anything different which can benefit me. By seeing a millionaire's son or daughter we used to think that, if our parents were a millionaire then we would be living a life of dream. Now a days, I used to think. If my mind used to work for me then I would be living an entirely different life. But sadly it's my mind who don't work for me. Even if I know, I hold the responsibility to mould my mind to this way.

So today I have decided to kill all those forces inside me who works against me. I don't want to have traitors within me. The best way to do it is to kill the current me and work to acquire the new me whom I dreamed of.

I don't want to live an ordinary life throughout my life or at least remove the tag of a loser from my forehead. I don't know how to change my current path. A path on which I am travelling for so many years can't be changed so easily. Its like a train in the railway track, where the train have only two options. go in front or go backward, apart from that they are not supposed or allowed to make a new move and for their entire life they follow the same path to and fro path. But a soldier in a chess by making a single square move can give a check to the king. He always moves straight but when seeing an enemy in the diagonal square he changes his move. After the move again travel straight. That should be my strategy. Go straight till my enemy comes near me. Wait for it and then plan the attack.

One thing I know for sure, if I don't act now. I will regret it for the rest of my life and I don't want to live with the pain of regret and don't want to wait till the point of time when I don't have an option to take a U Turn or to repair the damage I caused to myself. So the point is crystal clear in front of me. Fight till I beat the biggest beast in me and to give a clear message to myself and my mind. It's my way or the high way.

My Battle with me

It's a battle between me and myself. Sounds simple... yeah... believe me... it's not simple. My enemy knows me better than me. He knows my weakness, he knows my strength (which still now I don't know much), he knows the terrain of the war, he lives with me, understands everything about me, he can attack like a beast or can frighten me like a monster. He will make me feel like hell, he will play with my emotions. He will do anything to win the battle against me, he can take me to the edge of depression and still if he is not satisfied he can push me to commit suicide.

My mind projected all the fears within me

He always forced me live my life in fear, Fear of talking in public, fear of losing job, fear of being bullied, fear on living on passion, fear of losing comfort zone, fear of being rejected, fear of being neglected, fear of being omitted, fear of getting low appraisals, fear of not getting bonus, fear of getting negative feedbacks, fear of trying new thing, fear of wearing different dresses, fear of falling, fear of speaking English, fear of speaking my opinion, fear of sharing ideas, fear of living life with my terms and conditions, fear of being noticed, fear of being not noticed, fear of "what others think", fear of dying, fear of living, fear of dreaming, fear of coming second, fear of losing the race, fear of failing in exams, fear of god, fear of human and even fear of own reflection and shadow.

List of fears will goes on and on. A whole book can be written on the fears. Fear cannot be confined inside these pages.

It is not only my story. It's the story of an entire generation or humanity who think they are smarter and master of their mind. But in reality we all are slaves of our mind who is controlling us with all the fears. Fear is a good weapon by which anyone can be controlled. As we have read in history, emperors execute brutal and torture punishment for those who commit crimes or break law and go against the ruler. Punishment will be executed in public, so that the public see it and it develop fear within them and no one dare to commit crimes or to break laws or to go against the king.

My first step in the battle

Now I understand one thing. If I want to win this battle then I have to be better than current me for that I should understand myself. I should understand how my mind work and I should feel and think how my mind thinks and should understand the skills of negotiations which he does with me and what are the strategies which are in store for me. As my mind knows my weakness and my strength, I should also know my minds weakness and strength, so if he attacks me then I am ready for the counter attack. Want to make sure that the battle is fought between two equal opponent and till the last minute it's hard to predict who the winner is. One thing is for sure. This battle will last for a long time. But from morning wake up call to night sleep in call, I should be the one who should control the mind. Not the mind controlling me any more.

So I have to get rid of current me and transform myself to a better me. Here my journey starts , it's not an interesting journey at first glance. But the more you travel the more you enjoy and the more you enjoy the more you travel and for sure you will start loving the journey more than destination.

Does Motivation works in real life

I am a motivational speaker who is taking motivational and soft skill trainings for around five to six years. I love taking motivational sessions and by seeing my audience's expressions in the session, I think I am not bad at this job. At least I have the calibre and capacity to make my audience awake for two hour at a stretch of my session as a speaker. I think they are listening to me don't know, if I am wrong. Even if they are not listening to me, I don't mind. I know it's a task as difficult as climbing Mount Everest and writing your names on all the rocks at the top. Why I am telling is that, when I attended any Seminars and meetings, it takes me half an hour to go to sleep. Definitely not because of the Presenters or Speakers fault, I can't open my eyes for more than half an hour If I am continuously sitting in one position. You won't believe it, I don't go to watch movies either. No matter How good the movie is, I will sleep in half an hour and wake up at Interval and then I will come with a solid plan of buying Pop Corns and Cool Drinks which can make me sit and watch movie and not make me sleep. Then starts eating and drinking. By the time it finishes my mind starts sending signals. Watching movies or sleep. Watching movies or sleeping, watching movies or sleeping. First two times, I will say. Watching the movie and for the third time, it's sleeping and I sleep till the end of the movie and after movie without any hesitation and with immense proud and putting an intellectual mask, I will say at least five to seven reason why the movie was not good. I am not paid for my comments but doing the same thing many of peoples are earning and they called themselves critics.

So as mentioned I was happy with my motivational classes, when I see the spark in audience eyes at the sessions and which used to make me happy. But I don't see any changes in them after the session in their life. Which engulf my happiness. We don't even bother to think what went wrong. We got motivated on the session and we used to think, Yes this is the moment I was waiting for. I got to change myself and be a new human being. In short, killing myself for better me moment as I would like to call it. But after 15 to 20 minutes everything change. The inspiration or willpower got from the session will be drained or leak out. Getting motivated for no reason and getting back to normal, of course for many reasons. I am in love with me, my love is my comfort zone. How can I leave my lover for any other goal in my life. It's too hard to do it. I believe, we fail in convincing our mind to change itself.

First of all, I don't believe the word motivation really exist in the real world. Now you might be thinking that, as a motivational speaker, I am telling I don't believe in motivation. It's like a doctor declaring in public that he doesn't believe in medical science or a scientist telling he don't believe in science. How insane it would be. But that's the fact. I bet, can you show a single person whose life got transferred by hearing a motivational speech or by watching a motivational movie. It's very rare. Motivational speeches has the capacity to convince our mind, it has the power to think beyond our thinking, it has the power to show dreams and it has the power to give us goose bumps, but these are temporary feelings or emotions. It will not last longer.

It's like a motivated smoker telling himself that this is my last cigarette and after this I will quit smoking. But after an hour or two again he will smoke by making any excuse. An alcohol addict swears in the name of god and his children that he will quit alcohol consumption after fully drunk and next day he will repeat the same after drinking.

So the pivotal question remains unanswered. If motivational speeches or motivational movies or videos can't change you and your mind then what is the next plan.

So do I have to live my entire life hoping everything will be changed automatically or by seeing my pathetic situation God will come and give me three wishes or I will get a magical lamp with a geni inside it. If we got the three wishes also, I am sure it will be money, life style change or make me the more handsome and charming person in the entire world. That time also we will not ask to change the mind set or give me power to change myself and achieve the goals one by one or some super natural power will work for me or work on becoming Spider man over night by getting a bite from spider. In my childhood days I used to search for the spider who can make me spider man as many of the kids do. Or I have to accept the fact that I am just an ordinary person in life and live an ordinary and repetitive life everyone though out my life

When you decide to change yourself is the starting point which requires courage and energy from inside but to stick with your plan requires thousand time more energy and will power. Each and every minute our mind will try to find excuse for not doing it and if we are able to overcome that moments then we are nearing to our goal but at any moment we allow our excuses to overshadow our goal then the entire bridge you build between your current you to the new you will be broken completely. If you entertain one excuse at any point of time then everything will go in vain.

One example I would like to share regarding this point. When I take classes after one and half hour there will be a break of 15 minutes and for first few sessions I will ask the audience to come after 15 minutes. I tell them the exact time that should be back and I always see that after 15 minute just half of the audience will be available in the hall and rest everyone will come afer 20 or 25 minutes.

So I planned to do an experiment on it. Before the break I tell the group that you should be back to the hall by this time. Those who are coming late will have to sing or dance and I will ask each and every one to accept it verbally in front of every one so that no one can deny it. By end of 14th minute everyone is present in the hall. So what the difference happen here is that I have given them a goal which doesn't have any loop holes or have any excuses. If I am alive and you are alive and this hall stand same after 15 minutes without any change you have to sing or dance. No escape from it. So this was a straight goal without any exceptions. Its like do or die. No one want to sing or dance so no one wasted a single minute. Everyone utilized there 15 minutes completely and not a single minute is wasted.

Our problem is that we are good at planning but it would be like the break of 15 minutes, which you come within 15 minutes its okay if you come after 20 to 30 minutes it would also be okay. No one will question you. So why should I come in 15 minutes when I have the liberty to come at my own sweet time. This is what our mind will think, if it's a lose goal but a goal with a timeline is much powerful where your mind is convinced that you can't break the timeline and there is no other way to break timeline. Then see the magic. The same mind which will pull back you saying that there is more time for you to meet the deadline will work hard and its full potential so that you can achieve the goal. That's the moment you can tell I am controlling my mind. But we always ask the question to everyone why am I not able to do anything in life or why am I not successful.

I would say the question is asked by you and the answer lies inside you. We are trying to find the answer everywhere. We attend motivational sessions, we do yoga or meditations or do Google search and find a million activities ourselves. Go to temples, churches and mosques but never realize that the answers to all my questions, all miseries, all my sadness, all my depressions and all the negative vibes in and around me is within me. I am the answer to all the questions which I have. Its my ability to accept the challenge and the ability to fight with the situation will take me to the next level and more than that fight with the entire world to make my dream a reality. Its nothing but fight fight fight.

Our goals should like the person who don't know how to swim but is pushed to deep river or sea. There he won't say, "I don't know how to swim so I am giving up my life" and silently and quietly go inside the water with a smiling face. No, right. He will swing his hands and legs and do everything he can to save himself. He will fight with death and do everything possibility he can to save himself. There he will fight without having a second opinion or having an excuse.

Have you heard of the Musk Dear, it searches the source of the nice fragrant in jungle for his entire life, till it's last breath it doesn't understand that the fragrance it's searching is coming from it's own body. Same with us too. Look inside you instead of looking outside for the solutions. If you can't save yourself no one in this world and even god can't save you.

So always believe in yourself and believe in your dreams then see miracles will happen. It's a myth that everyone says Successful peoples have gods grace or they have some talent which I don't have. God has shown full justice to me and given me everything that those successful people have. Only difference is that they have used their weapon but I am still searching for mine.

I believe that, transformation happen from a positive mind set and a positive mind set comes with a positive mind and positive mind comes from a happy and blissful soul. So it's a reverse transition we have to work on. First step is to make your mind and soul happy and live a life by keeping perfect harmony with yourself.

Happiness and positive vibe

Being happy in the current world is a humongous job. We can find or explore anything in this world or we can get anything in the world which we dream of. We have found water in Mars planet, but to find happiness with in our self is very difficult.

Can you answer my simple question. When was the last time you were really happy. When I say happiness, it doesn't include happiness when you get a I-Phone as a gift or your friends or family throwing a surprise Birthday party. When was the last time you were happy without any outside reason?

External factors can make you happy for a short span of time and then it will pull you back to the normal or current state and to get short package of happiness we spend our entire life thinking these are the only happiness and beyond it there is nothing else.

What an irony, we work for happiness and we do everything to be happy. work hard only to be happy, spend extra time at office, busy with work, managing clients etc. But still we are not happy. We always think that today I will sacrifice myself, my family, my friends and work for happiness in future. So that tomorrow I can live a happy life with my family, friends and with myself. After years of hard work, when we decide to live life with happiness family and friends might have gone much far away from us and I will be left with myself. That time I will realise that I only know how to work for happiness which I have done for my entire life but I haven't taught myself how to be happy without doing anything. Then I pretend to be happy just to fool the entire world and myself, but I know that I am not happy and this will continue for the entire life.

Do you think working hard for entire year and then planning a trip with family for one week is happiness. Everyone including me think the same. But have you realize the value that you are paying for the trip. Its months of isolation from family and friends for five days and four night. Is it worth. Now we are living in a world where we have to buy happiness in form of family trip, outing etc, family dinner or movie. which certainly gives happiness, no doubt on it. but after that one week or two week everything is back to the same and then wait continue for next year or next family dinner or outings.

So now let's start our journey to find where we have missed our cute and bubbly kid called happiness. Journey back to many years. Back to our childhood days. Let's close your eyes and take one some steps back. One step can be one day or it can be one month or it can be one year. First thing I realized is that the graph of happiness getting more and more big when we step backward. Going really back in time will make you more and more happy. Our childhood days, the ground we play cricket, football etc and the road which where we waited for our crush and the tea stall where we have tea with our friends, Parents buying new cycle on birthday etc. So sweet time. Right

Now open eyes. Oh god. What a.. I don't know about you all. but sitting in front of the computer for hours, juggling between personal life and professional life. To add more misery in my life, I am writing this book in the middle of COVID – 19, where I am battling against a big monster in my life. WORK FROM HOME.

It mixed my professional and my personal life so much that now even I don't understand which is my personal time and which is my office time. In a perfect state of dilemma. Talking to clients by feeding my baby on my lap. It's good that my mobile, skype, Zoom and MS Teams have a mute function. Thanks to the technology. On a call of half an hour, I would have muted myself for more than 30 times to yell at my son and to fight with my wife or to say sorry. Me and my wife started thinking that our planning was wrong to have our second baby two years prior to COVID. By the time COVID knocked at the door of planet earth, he turns to be the most mischief kid in town. We used to think that a kid of one foot or two foot of height and 12 Kilo gram weight. A small package made two adults life miserable like hell. we both understand one fact of life. Size doesn't matter. A small stone is enough to break the window of the most beautiful mansion. All depends on the content inside the package. Our home is like the climax of Avenger movie where everything is destroyed from Airport to Sky scraper buildings, fields, houses everything and still the Avengers is fighting to save the city.

We are trying to find the minute drop of happiness which lies in the big mess and if you watch closely the minute drop of happiness is worth an ocean.

Just imagine how many fathers in this world have been blessed to be with their kids when they need you the most. To hug them, to pamper them, to take them for a ride and to hold and play, to hug them tight, to throw them on air and catch and hug them tight when they feel scared and look for someone. You are there for them. To see cartoons with your kid and to become a cartoon for your kid and play with them. I am one of the luckiest fathers who is living in the era of COVID and being with my kids not only at the week end but from start of the week to end of the weeks.

In fact nowadays, I feel happy to guide Dora and bujji to any mission and when she says "Do you see the mountain? If yes, Say mountain" and I would jump and say Mountain. Sometimes I feel like Dora is happy with my assistance and I enjoy seeing Chota Bheem eating ladoo. What a change in my life.

Before Covid, I felt that our life was like the old famous video game Super Mario where Mario runs and passes all the obstacles and takes all the pain and dies several times in between and come back with next life to rescue the princess, once he rescue the princess then the game is over. What the F****, Next day again I will run to rescue the princess and get the same message. Till now, the thought of living with the princess in an expensive Castile as a king made me run like a donkey every day and obey what all my boss say and laugh loudly at my boss stupid jokes, at time of laughing you realise that you are the biggest buffoon in this earth to laugh at the joke which was so out dated joke that our ancestors from Stone age will throw stone on these jokes. Started the run with a dream and now after so much years of running with out any result or without getting the princess. Now running without any reason or goal. Its part of my life and happily running. A journey from dream land to no dream zone.

Now come to the point, if we go back to our time. We can see we were more happy in our earlier days, When we were at college. Life was very colourful. It's like a set of Karan Johar movies. Bright colours everywhere. We feel like we are the Shahrukh khan and girls will do anything to get our attention. Spend a good time grooming ourselves and sometimes in Gym too. Time when we feel proud of our selves. Even the same I used to feel. When I watched "Kaho Na Pyar Hai " movie. I used to think I was the same as Hritik Roshan. Me and Hritik Roshan have many similarities. He is around 6 feet and me too.

What else. that's enough for me. In short we were very happy.

In our school life, small moments, small incidents and the good time spent with friends makes us happy. There is nothing to be sad of. Except the day when we get the answer sheet after exams. But anyways it's a part and parcel of the game. But that also won't made me sad. Along with me, if my friends fails, then I don't have any issues. If my friends pass and I failed then I feel sad. But thank god for giving me such good friends who always were with me in good and bad times. God has given me a good friend circle where I didn't get an opportunity to be sad for the above mentioned reason. There also life was very happy.

Going a little more back, when we were babies. It's hard to remember those days. But when you watch a baby, you can realise, that small toddler is happy without any reason. When I look from my angle. I feel insane . how can one be happy without any reason. If you give a baby a red colour toy, the baby is happy. if you give him a green colour toy he is happy or if you give a colourless toy, he is still happy. He will be happy by talking to himself. It feels like the baby is enjoying his life to the fullest.

Explore what you have

Why is the baby enjoying every moment. The answer is simple, the baby is happy with what he has and the baby doesn't have set any expectation or conditions to be happy. The problem which we have is, we are not happy with what we have in hand and running behind we don't have. Once we get what we want then we will take that as granted and never care for it much.

Some years back to own a smart phone is a dream of every one. To hold the sleek phone and touch the screen and watch videos on it and do all those crazy things which we dreamed of. But after owning the mobile the joy of owning the mobile decrease tremendously. Just one week after, it will become just a normal gadget in our life and we start dreaming for some other thing and this one in hand looks very cheap. A journey of a dream to scrap at very fast pace.

We expect more from life and in the business of expectation and reality, we miss to live our life. We are stuck between the expectation and reality. In reality we dream of expectation and when we meet expectation with a couple of days or with in a week, the fantasy will drop and again came to ground zero of reality. We believe in running and catching dreams and what about the dreams which we have already cached or we had with us. Before getting demotivated or upset for the things that we don't have, just look around you and be happy with what you have. With the available resources around you, you can achieve much bigger dreams. By doing that we will start enjoying each and every moment.

For example, you have a bad day in office and with all the frustration in mind you come to home and your kid with happiness comes to you and start bugging you to take them out or to buy ice cream or chocolate. We will yell and blast at them and take out all our angry frustration on them.

But now turn the table and look the same scenario from other angle. You had a bad day at office you reach home and the same kid bugging you and instead of yelling at him, if you look at their face and see the love and the innocent smile and the happiness of seeing you after long hour, that the kid is expressing in his or her way and if you smile and hold them in your hands, give them a kiss and a tight hug and be with them for some time. I can bet with in 30 sec to one minute your mood will be changed completely. It's a big transformation and for the entire night you will feel relaxed. So give importance for what we have instead of worrying on what you don't have.

Be happy with what you have and believe me, happiness is the starting point of positive mind set and positive mind set is the key for a successful life.

Have you ever seen yourself at bad mood and getting new ideas or feeling awesome. It won't work that way. If you have a good positive vibe or a positive mind set then everything will fall in its place and your mind will start working for your dreams. So start enjoying the small drops of happiness in life. Even its not much. In short try to find small small happiness around you and live the happiness to the fullest. For that you should be having an open mind set to see everything around you in a multiple dimension. A closed mind set is like a watching beautiful destinations in the world in a black and white TV. Where we believe that world around us is full of black and a little bit of white. Its all about changing the setting of our mind then we can realise that what we think is dark and black is actually a 4K colour destination. Then we start enjoying every moment of it.

Setting conditions to be happy

Coming to the next point, Now we are on the edge of humanity. We all are busy in running races and being happy is nearly to impossible and its far thing to dream of. Being human is the biggest favour that we can do to our self in this current world. A complete transformation from Yash Raj movie with colourful overseas locations and romantic songs to Anurag Kashap movie.

You know where we have missed our happiness and the positive vibes or the positive energy. We started putting more and more conditions to be happy. When we were babies, there were no conditions in our life. So for any small reasons we used to smile or without any reason we used to be happy. At the time the school conditions were limited, so we were happy. Even in college we live without much condition.

Now we are a multi-national factory of conditions. We are like China who is never satisfied with the existing borders. Want to extend borders more and more. Same like we are adding more and more conditions to our lives and making it more and more complicated. To add conditions, we have convinced our mind by giving clear instructions; unless these conditions are not met don't make me feel happy. Here the culprit is not the mind. We are the culprit, mind is just running the program which we have coded deliberately or unknowingly.

If we want to live a happy life, we should break or delete many of the conditions. I won't say all, but many of the unnecessary conditions should be uninstalled from our mind.

When expectations are more, being happy is more difficult. Day in and day out we are fighting with ourselves and with the world to satisfy our expectations and at the end of the fight, suppose if we are able to satisfy our expectations then also our happiness will be limited for some time. We can't extend it, the boundary of happiness ends when next condition comes to play. These conditions are much stronger than happiness. Conditions can seriously reduce the life of happiness. In theory, happiness lives in the mercy of conditions and that happiness we are working for day in and day out, put all our efforts and spend an entire life is a supressed by our own conditions and we think that our efforts are not getting transformed to happiness when we work extra hours and put more burden on our self. By working hard we are making money and putting it in Fixed Deposit for future and unknowingly our happiness is also on a Fixed Deposit plan and till now we don't know the maturity date of it . We are good at planning our retirement but we are bad at planning today.

We build big houses or buy expensive flats to make our self happy and to live a happy life. One month later when the EMI starts then all our happiness are gone and for next twenty years we are haunted by bank and lenders. It's not necessary to be live in a big or expensive house to be happy. It's a condition we have kept in our mind. A small house with over joyed members is far better than a big house with gloomy or sad members.

It's like receiving an appreciation email in our Mailbox from our boss for the hard and dedicated work done for days will make you happy till there are four or five more emails came over it. It has only the value of the newspaper which will be sold like a hot cake for the day but for next day it's just a waste paper. It's value is only for 24 hours.

So just imagine we are sacrificing our happiness, personal life, friendships and to be happy for 24 hours and we are not even happy for 24 min in a day or a week. Is it a fair deal to be signed?

We always watch movies with an expectation and if the director fails to make the movie to our expectation then we curse the director, actors, producers, theatres and even our friends who have taken the ticket for the movie for wasting our three hours. Suppose if we watch a movie without any expectation then just imagine we will start clapping and get Goosebumps on 90s Tamil and Telugu action movies. The local low budget horror movies will look like blockbusters. then you can watch all movies without checking its rating or reviews. Just imagine how cool is that.

Do you remember the 90's, when Doordarshan was the hottest trend and we used to watch the regional language movies which come on every Sunday afternoon. I don't know about you all. But I watched almost all the movies and no prizes for guessing, most of the languages used to fight with each other to give their best of the best slow and the boring to hell movies. (No offense to Doordarshan, nothing on you) After watching those movies it takes some time to recover from the 3 hour of trauma. After knowing that next week also it will be the same story, I used to sit in front of my Black and White TV. Life was so cool and colourful, because I was not expecting anything from the movie or from Doordarshan. Same me cannot watch a movie, if any of my friend say any negative comments. If it get 3.5 to 4 starts then only we will start thinking of watching movie and if its not good then we think it's a waste of time.

The heights of expectations are like watching and enjoying a suspense movie and if it's climax doesn't turn out to be as good as we expected, we would not like the movie at all, even if till climax the movie makes you sit at the edge of the seat. On a two and half hour of movie, when the last five minute were not good, how good it would be to tell that "it was not up to my expectation".

Come on guys, we have to do something about the Cancer called expectation which is slowly taking away happiness and still now I am not realizing and it's spread is at a high level and becoming incurable. If I don't do anything now, there will be one day I will forget what happiness is and at that time I have to pay a huge price for happiness and by that time, I will not be in a position to pay it. Because I might have lost everything which used to be there in my world. My family, my friends, my parents, my sweet house, my kids.

I am currently learning art to kill 'expectations'. You can enrol for my new course for just $499. Limited seats available. If you join now, you will get a discount of $50.

Don't fall into the trap. No one can save you. You have to save yourself. Have you ever noticed a mad man on the road side, sitting near the drainage with dirtiest look and dress, eating thrown foods from waste bins. It might be the most unpleasant site for us. But next time when you see a man like that, just watch him for some minute. What all he does, He enjoys doing it. There are no conditions or expectations for him. He lives life in his own conditions and when he looks from his point of view. He finds the entire world is insane and he is only the perfect creation of god and which god is proud of.

So why can't we try to live like that. Not an insane life. Just live a life without much expectation.

Like when we wake up in the morning. Instead of saying, oh god today also it's raining or today also it's hot or cold and then going to the bathroom. Why can't we open the windows and watch nature for some minutes and cherish the wonderful ambiance the nature set for us and then go to the bathroom. When the morning started with a positive note, same vibe will continue for the entire day. Next thing when coming to the dining table and seeing the upma or poha or idli and thinking "Am I staying in any rehabilitation centre where my diet is fixed by the doctors? 50% of it is fixed based on your health point and another 50% based on the sins I have done in the past".

If you remove the small small expectations before coming to the dining table, whatever be there as breakfast waiting for you, you will enjoy seeing that and eat from bottom of your heart and it will taste delicious and it will be blissful moment, in short from morning it'self you starting with a positive note and enjoying your life.

Do you know the water we drink? We drink water frequently as advised by Doctors that the human body needs around 8 litre of water daily. We started following it.

We always drink water but we never understand the taste of water. But when we are really thirsty and the thirst has reached it's edge. On that point, have you noticed the taste of the first drop of water that touches into our mouth? It would be the most awesome moment of your life. Nothing would have refreshed you more than the tasteless water. when you see the water in front of you. The same water we drink just to satisfy the quota of 8 litre.

At that time we didn't understand the value of water. But the moment you understand the value of water, you will respect water and you will drink water with enjoyment and the moment you start to drink or eat anything with enjoyment , body and mind will accept it whole heartedly. it will have a positive effect on the body too. In turn you will be having a perfect harmony between mind and body and positivity will start from there.

Respect each and every thing. Even if it's a bitter gourd or bitter guard curry which your mom has made for you. Eat with the same enjoyment which you show while eating Chicken and mutton. Basically, it's not what's in front of the table that should activate your taste buds but it's your respect towards the food which activates the taste buds in the dining table.

This I am writing from my experience. I also had many conditions about food. But it was till 10th standard. After that I was in a hostel in Nagpur, Maharashtra in North India and I have ate some of the most disastrous food in the planet and understood the value of home cooked food. From that day till now, I never had a problem at the dining table. What all I get, I eat with full heart.

I even like what I cook too. Because when you know, there can't be anything worse than this. Then you realise all your moments till now were the best moments of life. That's the moment of enlightenment. Everyone gets this lesson in some or other manner. But only some take it as a valuable lesson and others will ignore it. But those who take it as a valuable lesson and adapt it to life, they will never fail in life. You know why, there is no condition set for failure.

As Edison said, once he was asked by a reporter that "You failed around 1000 times for making a bulb. How would you see that".

He told, I never failed. I learned 1000 methods by which bulbs cannot be made. If the failure is not in your list of condition then it's only learning, not failing.

You might not believe it, if I say. Nowadays I started enjoying, when my wife shouts at me. Previously we used to have frequent fights for most important things in our life. On those things which have the gravitas to change our lives completely from head to toe. Like I am not keeping the pillows and bed sheets in order after sleep, I sit for long time in loo, I don't know how to use the toothpaste correctly, sometimes there will be toothpaste sticking in the washbasin, stains and food particles are not removed when I wash dishes and utensils, I wear same dress for more than a day, I don't keep things at it's place after using it, I make the worse tea and many more. Earlier I got irritated and lost my temper. Now I started seeing things differently.

She looks more pretty when she is angry and the words coming from her mouth is like a Honey Singh singing a rap song or Usha Uthup singing a pop song. The dialogues, sentiments and the quantity of emotions she put to make the moment possible is tremendous. I feel like, she is a natural actress who starts living in the character and pays 100% justification to the role.

Those who are married, just try this. I am sure next time you will invite her to start a debate and enjoy it to the maximum. I bet it. Moral of the story, the quick you learn this skill the better you start enjoying your life.

So in short, identify your expectations at all points of life. If possible note it down. Break the expectation. It's difficult but practice it daily and within 15 to 20 days, all it takes to get rid of the extra conditions and expectations which are standing between you and your happiness. Extra luggage are always a problems, even if it's a trip or it's life.

Why I am stressing more on happiness, is that. When you are happy, there will be a positive vibe in you and what all jobs you do with positive energy and with positive mind set will give you positive result for sure. It's the law of nature the effort you put will come as a result to you. If you put your positive energy it will give a positive result. If you put negative energy.

So the solution to the problem is to free your happiness from conditions and the most important thing, don't create a link or relation between happiness and conditions. Both are separate entities and have its own importance in our life. It should be unconditional happiness and let live a better life and in turn it will give a great pleasant and happiness in your life too.

Looking at the clock I realize that I am sitting in front of this laptop for more than two hour. For me it's a record. Even at work and studies, I don't sit in front for more than 45 min to max one hour. It's time for a break. Without any expectation I am going to make a tea for myself and I will surely try to enjoy it. Will continue if I am alive or healthy after the tea break. Stay tuned for more action in upcoming pages.

Respect Time

Just imagine the years you lived your life. Procrastinating all your tasks for tomorrow and dreaming for a better future. It doesn't work that way. Suppose on a fine day, you went to a doctor for a regular check-up and after half an hour seeing your doctor with the seriousness in his face, tells you that you will only live for one more week. You have left with a week. Then how will you live that week. You have two options left with you. Put yourself in a closed room and live with sorrow, depression and guilt or live the week to the fullest. I would prefer the second option. Because at that time you know the value of time. Every minute and seconds count.

Have you ever run a marathon or run on a tread mill by setting time of half an hour or fifteen minutes. At that time we realize the value of time. Every seconds count. We look at the watch and calculate ten more minutes, nine more minutes and the last one minute will feel like the biggest one minute in our life. There we realize how time works and we can see how slow time it's moving. Its dragging. That moments we respect time and for rest of the day we don't much respect time as everything we take it as granted. Theory of time is very simple. Give respect to time and time will respect you otherwise don't expect.

I was in Dubai for around 7 years. When I come back home for vacations and when I realize only one week is left for my vacation and I have to fly back to Dubai. I still remember, I live that one week to the fullest. As I know once I land in Dubai, my life will be a mechanical one. Work, home, work, home. Nothing more.

So I try my level best to live that one week to the fullest. So that I don't regret when I touch the land of Dubai.

My point is, Live life daily as it's your last day of your life and then you will see the difference. You will start enjoying your life to the fullest and you will find limited time to accomplish your goals. So you will work faster and harder and in turn you will develop a system and mind which will respond to your call instantly on your instruction. There wont be any room for sadness, grievances or to be negative as your entire day is booked for all productive activities and at the end of the day you will feel the vibe of achievement and you will understand the great potential in you by which slowly you will start loving yourself. Once you start loving yourself then you can do anything or to go any extent to make yourself happy.

For example, we have planned a trip with our friends and the night before the trip when we go to bed and set an alarm for 5AM. Next day , I bet we will wake before 5AM and turn off the alarm, even if we had gone to bed at 3AM. Suppose the same Alarm set for work purpose or for study. At least for three to four times it will go for snooze and then after all the struggle we will wake up two to three hours later then the set time.

All it matters is the importance is the goal or our plan. If our mind identifies it as a plan which involves emotions and sentiments then it will react to it with the same intensity and when we set a plan without putting our emotions into it then our mind will react to it in the same way.

At the start of the day, when you wake up. You should have the Time table for the entire day. You should be able to visualize the entire day at the start of your day itself. Doing all the important or tough work at the start of the day, when you are filled with energy and keeping all the easy and simple jobs to the end of the day. Prioritize the work by keeping in mind that you have only 24 hours and 1000 works are pending. So the most priority should be completed first. Spend your energy wisely in productive activities which is an important aspect. With an example I will explain it.

Suppose you have a car and the mileage of car is 20KM/Litre and you have only one litre of petrol in the car. Which ever direction you go or where ever you go, the maximum distance you can cover is 20 KM, if it's a hilly area or road with full of bumps then it will be reduced to 15 or 16. Inside city you will get a maximum of 13 to 15 KM/Litre but you will never get a mileage more than 20KM with one litre unless and until you work on the engine or related part.

On every day, when we wake up we only have a limited energy which can drive ourself to 15 or 50KM. it purely depend upon the activities that we do on a daily basis. If you wake up and spend a good amount of time on Watsup, Facebook or Instagram a percentage of energy is drained there without any productive result and then for all activities you do in a day with the small percentage of energy which is left out. When the fuel tank is empty then you will feel the tiredness and that's the moment you understand no I can't work more and should relax.

Just imagine, you are spending a good amount of energy in watching TV, mobile or browsing on internet regarding some stupid topic which doesn't have to do anything with you, that mean you are wasting the fuel for the day which your body and mind stored for you expecting to something good to you and we simply waste it thinking that "it's my time and I know how to use it".

Most of the genius people don't even talk much, as they believe in saving the energy which may have lost due to talking. For walking, running and doing all activities we need energy and my friends, all the energy our mind and body is taking from this fuel tank. So talk when it's required so that you can concentrate all your energy on one point, to satisfy your dream.

Second problem is that, when we start doing something our mind will try to give a list of 1000 + excuses for not doing it and we usually fall in the trap of mind. Here comes the 10 to 15 min technique.

Have we ever noticed that when you start your work for the day, we sit and login to the computer with least interest. There is no motivational factor which drive me to do the work. The only factor which drive me to do my work is "it's my bread and butter and I don't want to die starving". But when you start doing work with in 15 min you slowly start gaining interest and the graph of interest and concentration increases with every minute pass and the energy starting flowing on a single point and it becoming more powerful. We will enjoy the moment of work when there is no distraction and we are fully concentrating on single point. Then the famous universal bell curve theory applies. The concentration and interest will reach to the maximum and slowly it will come down to the ground where it has started it's journey. That's the time your mind cry for a break.

So my point is, forcefully concentrate for 10 to 15 minute and then our mind will take care of rest one or two hour. So what is my investment. 10 to 15 minute and my return will be a productive one or two hours. Super deal.. right.

Next point, how to gain interest on doing something passionately other than watching movies.

I will tell you a small example. Many of us might have gone to the gym to make a perfectly toned body and look like John Abraham or Rock. But after starting the gym around 80 to 90 percentage people quite gym in a month or two. After one week when they look at their body, they realise that not a single cell in the body has changed and only one thing has increased, that is pain. When you analyse the situation, you realise that Pain to sacrifice the sleep, Pain to get up from Bed, Pain to go to Gym, Pain of running on tread mill, Pain of taking the weight and the pain of taking the extra weight when girls are near you in gym. Now the option to choose from is clear. Get friendship with the Cosy and relaxing matters on the bed or have friendship with heavy duty gym equipment. Without wasting a single second the 90 to 95% chose the first option and happily live their life as they live till now, but the 5 or 10 % are the one who chose the hard part because they only see the end result, they don't see the pain. They walk, talk, sit, sleep with the dream in their eyes and they can only see the toned body they made. That's the level of passion they are addicted into.

So the point is that, when you see the path it may be difficult and will often drag you back from doing the work but when you start dreaming about the end result and that's become your point of motivation, no one will dare to whisper on your ears that the task is difficult, better to quit. So whenever you dream of anything, work on just thinking on the end result not on the painful or bumpy roads which lead to the destination and always be ready to face the worst situation and be alert as there are many invisible or visible entities all over the places who want you to quit.

You will find enough fuel to drive extra mile. That's what I called, work on the engine to improve the mileage of the car. When you know you have limited fuel and you have unlimited things to do in life, so the best option is to work on the engine and revamp yourself. If you only concentrate on road then it would look difficult and boring and after some day you will lose interest in the drive. But if you look at the destination and find the destination as a dream come true destination then road won't bother you. How bumpy the road might be, you don't care. Ups and down will not stop the enthusiasm of the drive. Your mind will be so synchronised with your body that you won't feel the pain and if you feel the pain too. You will start enjoying the pain.

So everything who you dream should start with a dream in mind and the dream is so deeply rooted that dream should drive you. The famous quote of Abdul Kalam Azad "A dream is not what you see at sleep, a dream should be something which wont let you sleep". Truly motivating words.

Always be motivated for no reason. If I get a million dollar or if I lose a decent amount in Tax my motivational level should be the same.

So next big question, how to dream or how to build the passion which drive us. It's difficult. Many of us living a normal life for years and if I tell you one day that you have to build a dream and work with passion to achieve the dream then it would sound like a fairy tale , where you kiss a frog and your fortune changes or rub the magical lamp and you are a proud owner of a genie. But the real life doesn't work that way. We identify dream and for some days we work for the dream and then slowly moves to the current state of mind. It's like a tug of war. We try to push our self forward but many of the unknown or known forces are pulling us backward. So what should be done to move forward with the dream. I would like you to be my guest to the next topic.

Emotional Power

Have you ever heard of the Emotional Power. I don't know, if I am sounding insane. But from my point of view, it's the most important weapon one should acquire and believe me it's the most lethal weapon. When selecting or working for a goal, make sure that you are attached to the goal emotionally as I told earlier. The more you are attached emotionally with your goals the more result you will get it. It's about convincing your mind to work for the plan which you really feel is important for you.

In life there are two plans which are available, Plan A and Plan B and after that we also know there will an endless series of plan for a same task. If Plan A fails, we have Plan B and if Plan B fails we have Plan C and if Plan C fails then say goodbye to all plans and go to home and relax.

As a human tendency, we always have multiple plans which can be moulded to our conditions and which always provide the ease of work. We always have multiple choices which doesn't bother or care about deadlines. Simple theory. Deadlines are the lines which can be extended or crossed at our convenience. So if we are flooded with Plans, then why should I do hard work or dedicate my time and energy on Plan A when I knew that I have many plans, if this plan fail. In a situation, if you are given option then why should you waste your full energy on Option one. It will never come to your highest priority because you didn't make it to priority list.

Standing on shore of river, if you are asked to swim. You can say, "I don't know how to swim. Better than swimming, I will go for boating". But when you are thrown into water and you are drowning. Will you say, I don't know swimming. I prefer dying and silently close your eyes and wait for dead or you will try all your possible swimming moves or do everything to save yourself from drowning. You will put your heart and soul to come out of the situation. It's do or die.

That's how a plan work. When you know that there is no Plan B for me as a backup. You will give your 150% of effort to make the Plan A work, but the moment you know that there is a Plan B. then you wont even put your 50% of effort.

I understand this point when I was in college. At Board exams we used to study religiously and with the fullest of dedication and extreme efficiency, because, if I fail in Board my life is finished. One year waste is a secondary thing. The entire society would look as if you are the Serial killer in the town walking on the road and you have been convicted for murdering a dozen of pretty girls in the town. So no option is left other than to pass the exam and that also with good numbers. So put my heart and soul to it. 15 to 20 hours I have studied and at collage we have a supplementary. If you fail in final exam, you will be promoted to next year and within two three months there will be one more exam, on that you can clear it. So when I got option, I am completely relaxed as I know. If I failed also nothing will change as I have a second chance. So the mind-set is entire different. The view regarding the exam is completely changed.

When ever we give a second option to our mind. The mind will understand that the Plan A is not that important as there are series of plans.

Now coming the Emotions. As I mentioned earlier that emotions hold high power. It can make us do anything. It can make us do things which we never thought we would ever done in our wildest dream.Emotions are the most powerful tool we have. It can create wonders and it has the capacity to boost you to the next level. With one example I will be able to convince you the power of Emotions.

When I was in Dubai, there was a fire accident near my residence where I lived. It was a villa where one or two families lives. The fire was uncontrollable and every one was watching it and waiting for the Fire force to come. First time in my life I was seeing a scene like this. Believe me, it was scary. The kitchen of the Villa was facing at the front and we can clearly see the kitchen and what added more tension to the situation was, we can clearly see a Gas cylinder from the window. The situation become more tense, if someone didn't take the Gas cylinder out of the kitchen then surely there will be a blast and I don't know what would be the impact of it and what would the causality that can have. As it's the residential area with a decent population and many spectators came to watch the file. Every one was tensed and no one know what to do. Suddenly one guy from nowhere, went inside and took the Gas cylinder and ran out. Every one was watching in shock and the entire crowds mouth is wide open. That was the bravest act I have ever seen in front of me. He successfully taken the Gas cylinder from the villa.

I went to the guy and people were praising him, hugging him and congratulating him and I can see his hands and full body was shivering. When people were thanking him and asked him, how did you do it. Are you not afraid of fire, some thing could have happened to you. he told that " I lives in the next villa and I have a four month old baby in my villa along with my wife. If the gas cylinder bursts then it would be a situation I can't imagine". He was not able to speak and tears were coming from his eyes and he was not able to control his emotions. Till that time, I thought that it was an act of courage but now when I see his eyes. I can see the fear of a father and a husband. I was seeing a true father and a husband in front of me. Who was ready to sacrifice his life for his baby and wife. It's a moment of thought and you don't see anything else. Only your goal and the single moment when you realise the goal is bigger than life and to achieve the goal, if life should be scarified then also it's not a bad deal.

So the point is, if the fire would have caught somewhere else. This man will never think of throwing himself towards fire to get the Gas cylinder out. He never would have imagined it in his wildest dream. When his emotion, his baby and wife comes into picture and when he relates the adverse situation by linking his emotion then he gets immense power and his fear becomes his strength and his emotions were so powerful that he was not seeing the fire that is between the man and the Gas cylinder. He was only seeing the Gas cylinder and the mission statement was very much clear. Get the Gas cylinder outside the kitchen at any cost. He don't even think of the pain of getting in the fire or he didn't even thought of losing life in the act.

That's the power of Emotions. Suppose if we tag our goals with the emotions what would the extra power we will get from it. It's an deadly combination. In school days, when teacher embarrass us in front of the class for getting low marks or not answering a simple question and everyone is laughing at you, including your crush, then that moment we will determine in our mind that next exam, I will top in the class and at night when we become lazy and not having any interest in studying or feeling bored of studying. By just recollecting the moment of humiliation and next minute all your emotions will start converting to energy. You will be like a powerhouse of energy and you can put your brain and heart to book for hours without any laziness and the next exam for sure you will top it, because the emotions made our mind and brain work for a single goal.

We have heard news of Indian Soldiers deployed in Searching or any other parts where the climate conditions are the most adverse. We used to think about what makes them survive in these adverse conditions. Is it the salary or the perks or the quota of rum they get every month or any other incentives. But the answer is, it's the emotions which drive them. Emotions towards their team or regiments and emotions towards the mother land. If their emotions dried down then they will look for some better opportunity. We might think that they don't have the opportunity to move, that's why they have to do what they are doing. Like, if we don't like the job what we are doing currently we can move to other organization which can give us job based on the skill set we acquire from the current organization. But in Army, if they don't like the job they can't quit job from Indian Army and join Pakistan Army or Srilankan Army. But it's completely wrong, these are men and leaders who can handle all the situation and they never run away from any situations. Men who didn't ran away when their life was in stake. These are people most of the organisations looking for. The skill set and strategies which they develop in their tenure is priceless. If these people don't have emotions, then Indian map would be in an entirely different shape. Their emotions made Indian Army, one of the toughest Army in the world.

So before executing any plans, try to put emotions to it. Tag Emotions and then start working on it. Instead of seeing the short term pains and obstacles and challenges, see the end result. I am investing my time in writing this book by imagining, I will get some prestigious award for best book published in the history of mankind or it will become a bestseller. I know it will never happen

But If I dream of an author of a bestselling book, then only my book will have one or two copy sale at least in our Residential Colony or I will get an appreciation, not by any of my reader but at least from my wife, who don't have any other option or I will get an appreciation at least by my 5 year kid, who can use this book to throw at the stray dog.

So if you have a goal in life, don't simply work for the goal. It would be like walking in a desert where you can only see sand and nothing else and after sometime you will be bored and quit walking. Goals without an emotion is like living in an abandoned town by your choice and blaming god that my life doesn't have any colour or excitement.

So put emotions and see the energy in motion will drive you. These emotions will never make you quite. If it's an abandoned village, your emotions will work with you to make it a heaven.

So ask yourself first, why should I do this. What is the benefit of investing a big time in what I think is my goal is, what I will achieve by doing this and many more questions to yourself and your mind will add emotions and colour to your goals. If you get it then make sure that flame of emotion should never lose fuel to burn.

One example I will tell. If I give you a book of 1000 page, a big book and that also without any photos or short stories and tell you read the book and when you ask me the question, "why should I read" . I would simply say. I am telling you read the book and you have to read the book. I don't know why, this book is good for General knowledge and you can improve your knowledge and this is not so interesting book, but it's a nice book. Will you ever read the book? I guess the answer is No. hopefully

But if I give you the same book and tell you to read the book and the same question you ask me "why should I read the book" and I will say. There is an exam coming next month for a job vacancy and all the questions will be from this book and no one knows about it.If you are selected the salary and perk for the job is awesome. Now will you read the book. Hopefully the answer is YES. I don't know about you, but for me it's one million yes.

Now I have a reason, goal filled with emotions and I will ran to my room and switch off my mobile and start reading the book with a ton of interest, the same book on my earlier scenario, you will read with a minimal interest and might have completed in one month or two or might never complete the book. But in the second scenario, you will put your emotions and all your energy in the book and for sure complete the book in a week.

So what did I tag to it. Awesome Job and awesome salary. Then everything changed. It's as simple as that. If you look life just like that, it look so boring. But when you add emotions then it would be more colourful. A transformation from black & white Television to a 60inch plasma TV. Always keep a vision. Which is much ahead of short term goals . The satisfaction it gives when achieved is immense. So make your goal your passion. I am sure it would be a different ball game. Then you will not climb the steps, because steps will only take you to the terrace or to the next floor. You will start flying which will take you to the open sky and then you will start finding more and more opportunities to fly higher and higher. So give your wings the power of emotions and mind the passion of the goal.

Confront with your Fear

Before revealing my next point. I want to create some suspense. Because I heard that Thriller and Suspense novels, stories and movies have more market value and everyone will stand in line to buy it. So I don't want to leave any stone unturned. My book should have drama, masala, romance, action, comedy, tragedy and many more emotions. So that if one didn't work. It should sell on others. Just kidding.

From childhood days we were not alone. There was a person or you can say an invisible entity who lives with us. When we get older and bigger that invisible entity starts growing along with us. But the only difference is that. It has grown double the size of us. Starting as a small pet now turns out to be a big monster. Most disappointing part is that it's getting bigger day by day and we are living at it's mercy.

It's none other than our fears. I am limited to what I am just because of my fear of trying new things. From our childhood days we only did what we were instructed to do and our elders injected a small dose of fear when we tried to do something different. Don't go outside Ghost will catch you, don't talk to strangers. They will kidnap you etc.

From my childhood days till now I am hearing, you should never get wet in rain. Keep yourself away from rain. Otherwise you will end up having a cold and fever and the same people used to say when I take bath in minutes, that you should pour more water in your body and clean it. Take your own time and have the luxury of using all the water in the bathroom. Both are water, one is coming directly from nature, other has already reached the earth earlier and is coming from a different source. the water coming from shower is good and the same water is coming from clouds is not good. One second of getting wet in rain will make you sick and five to fifteen minutes of getting wet under the shower will not. I don't know if there is any logic or any scientific fact in it. But one thing is for sure, from childhood I started to fear rain. Instead of enjoying rain, I start to run for shelter. The seed of fear put in my mind from my childhood is now a strong tree which will not allow me to go on rain and enjoy it fully. Fear in the sense, when I am watching rain from home I will enjoy it but when I am exposed to rain, I will fear. Fear for no reason.

Sometimes I used to think, from our childhood we have been restricted on many things. Don't do this, don't do that etc. in a day. If you start counting the Do's and Don't s , it ratio would be around 90:10. After 9 or 10 Don't we will hear one Do it. So slowly we started to fear doing anything new.

Once we fear doing anything, we will always stick to what we are doing now and our life will be like a train running in the railway track. Even if it's a bullet train or a Local passenger train, it can't think of taking an inch of deviation to left or to right. Same like that, we have set a boundary wall and will do only which falls inside the wall and unfortunately the boundary wall is very small. We will never try to trespass the wall, because the first emotion which comes to our mind is fear. Fear of doing anything new or anything different. But if you do it, we will never fear it again in your entire life. It's a matter of trying it once.

It was way back to my 20's. When I was working at a Call Centre at night shift and I used to travel by bus to my home. One day following the same routine I was coming by the bus and it was monsoon time and when I reached my home town and the rain was over and at 1.30AM or 1.45AM , I got out of the Bus. I used to off board the bus half a km before the designated bus stop to take a shortcut by which I can reach home faster and can save at least 15 min to 20 min. The shortcut I used to take is a quite silent road with no people and sometimes no street lights also, a little bit creepy road . That day as usual I was very much hungry and wanted to reach home superfast.

I started walking through the road and there was a turn and I was quite okay with no streetlights as there were enough lights from the homes near to the road. When I took the turn I saw something which had taken hell out of me and I was almost at the edge of panic attack. At the end of the road where the next turn is, there is a house and that house is exactly opposite to me and I am walking towards the house to take the next turn. I can see a shining white gown shining and hanging in the air and it was moving too.

It feels like some girl is watching me from the air and moving hands and the dress is also moving.

Just imagine a situation like that, where you are alone and you know some ghosts are there waiting for me near the turn. My hands were wet with sweat and my heart beat was so fast that I can hear and I am loosing my control over the body and had no clue what to do. My mind and brain was almost dead and then when my senses are back I realise that my body is walking without my instructions. I still don't know the motivation or objective of me waking towards the ghost. Might be my hunger or something else. I think at the moment my brain had taken a challenge with that witch. " You are hungry, I am hungry , let's see who's hunger wins tonight".

No idea. When I was nearing that ghost kind of thing my heart was beating like Jhankar beats which T Series was having in 90's songs.

When I almost reached it, I realised that it was not a ghost or a vampire or a witch who was waiting for me to suck my blood. Actually that was Light coming from a small window of the house on the first floor and in front of the house there was a tree and in a small wind the branches of the tree were moving and the mist around it gives it more original look. All these combined gives a perfect image of someone hanging in air, as the light coming through the branches and moment of the branches has given the special effects. Gives the feeling that the ghost was dancing too.

When I realised it, the relief I felt was immense. That moment I understand one thing. If I would have walked out or run back without facing the situation then in my entire life I wouldn't have gone through that road at night time and more than that I would have told all my friends and family members that I have seen a ghost on that road. Which might have spread like a wild fire and many people might have avoided the road. That incident will haunt me always and my fear would never have allowed me to go on that road at night.

After that whenever I see any road with less or no light in my entire life, this incident will come to my mind and it creates a big panic and the fear of that incident which was somewhere in my vague memory will start popping out and the fear will take control . My fighting mode will be engulfed by the fear mode and the fear of dark will rise more and I end up becoming more and more fearful.

But just facing the situation is a 10 to 20 second act, but it will create confidence to beat the fear and it will never try or have the capacity to beat my confidence.

Otherwise how confident you are, these moments have the strength to drain out all your confidence and leave you with nothing. It can even change your attitude also. It's the matter of seconds, how you react to the situation and that moment will be registered in your mind and it will act as a reference note for all the situations same like this and these incidence have a great influence on your nature and habits.

Sachin Tendulkar, the best batsman the world had ever seen and he had gone through all the toughest situations and faced the toughest bowlers in the world. But in his entire career he seems to have fear of batting at 90's. The man who faced the lethal bowling with full of confidence will get out by a simple ball bowled by a part time bowler when he is in 90's.

We have heard students committing suicides just because they fail in the exam, is it the worst incident which our entire society is responsible for. Children's are always considered as an asset to cover up the incompetency of their parents. For example, I am not able to become a doctor or an engineer or an IAS or IPS Officer, so my child should become. I am not able to top Board or University exam, so my child should top it.

My child was not there in the world when I was playing or enjoying with my friends before the exams or I am having deep sleep on the night before exam. To cover up my mistakes which I made in my teen age my child should do the sacrifice of his or her good times by going to tuitions or entrance coaching. Exams are always showcased as parents face value or parents goodwill which society do the assessment on. If your child had good marks, you have a value in the society. Your stock will be at bull run and when your child fail then he is like an anti-social element who was born to waste money of parents and he is good at nothing. Students' calibre are only just judged in this parameter called exam. A three hour of paper will judge 365 days of your hard work. The fear of failing started from our childhood. Failing in sports, failing in exams, coming second or not getting prizes in art or cultural activities, failing in completing homework on time, failing in interview, failing in answering questions asked by Teacher in the classroom. We have always seen failure as a dark horrible world which is full of shame, sympathy and low self-esteem, looser tagged. A dark world which we are dragged into. But only some come out of it. If I started fearing the fear of failure. The failure will fear me always and I will never come out of the fear of failure. But I would love to see the world of failure with a different perspective. Then half of my fear will be conquered.

We should have a plan B for our children from childhood days onward, which we always forgot or deliberately ignored to pass to our children. What to do when you fail. We use to tell them, if you pass we buy watch, X Box game or an expensive cycle etc. but what if you fail. Then what we will do that they don't know. One of the factor of fear is facing an unknown situation. If the situation you already been into, you will never fear that much. But a situation you are not into or the situation you are facing for first time will fear you the most. If it's an adverse situation.

I have decided that, if my son fails in exam or have any failure in life and if he comes to me with heads down and stand in front of me with a sense of fear and shame then I will hug him and say.

Don't worry, it's not the end of the end. It's only a milestone which was not so good but you can do it buddy and I am with you and I trust you completely and I will show the same enthusiasm and energy which I showed him when he passed exams with decent numbers and do whatever it take to bring back the positive vibes in him.

If I beat him or scold him and leave him alone in the situation he will struggle a lot to come out of it and on every exam he will study with fear. Fear of failure, humiliation and the negative reaction from parents and when year pass by his mind will be same like a pressure cooker which can burst at any time. But if I hold his hand at the time of failure, he will understand that failure is not a bad thing. It's a learning curve and he will try hard next time not under pressure but with determination to prove himself and to prove that the trust I showed to him was not gone in vain. To prove this he will go to any extend and when he pass the exam, he will surely run towards me and proudly show the progress card and he will definitely say "Thanks Dad". Will there be any proud moment more than this in any fathers life. I don't think so.

It's not that hard, sit with your son or daughter diagnose the issue, identify the grey areas which or the pivot points which was got unnoticed and prepare him or her for the next battle. I don't expect my son to be a genius. I was an ordinary student in my academics and wife was too. So bloody hell, how can my son be extra ordinary. If he is an extra ordinary student, I will doubt on my wife. Just kidding.

So whenever he wins a battle, it's not his win alone. It's my win too. Here, what was my investment? Just some patience and control on my emotions and looking things from a different perspective. With the small investment my return is very high. I was able to develop a fighting spirit attitude in my son's nature. Now I am damn sure. He will never commit any act to end his life, if he fails. He will rise up and fight with more energy. He will fight again and again till he tastes the success. It can take one day, one week, one month or one year. But he will fight till he gets there.

Have we ever noticed that till the first two to four years of our life. we didn't fear much. As a baby we never feared the dark, never feared any ghosts or never feared thieves. Even kids don't even fear spiders on the wall. Super cool, isn't it.

Then after four years when we start developing common sense all the nonsense starts developing along with it. It's our parents who first program fear into our hardware by putting all sorts of fear to ease their job. "Beta (son) Eat quickly otherwise Gabbar will come", don't go in the dark, otherwise ghost will come". At childhood days when our imagination is at it's peak level, we have been imagining about how Gabbar looks like and what Ghost will do at day time and all that nonsense. By night slowly we start accepting that if I go out ghost will come and we start to fear the dark. Till now, if we hear a pin dropping sound in the dark. We will fear. Matter of fact is we never seen a ghost in our entire life, but still we fear of ghost.

Still now when I am on my bed and I look from my window. I feel someone is outside and will peak now from the window. Of Course without telling you might have understood.

Our mind is a fertile soil for fear. You put any seed of fear. Big, small anything. our mind will accept the seed of fear and make a big tree out of it. Small small seeds which have been put in our mind from our childhood days are the biggest trees of fear we have now. Now our mind is like a rain forest of fear. We fear almost everything. We proudly say that we control our mind. But the matter of fact is that our fears control us.

I would blame my teachers who had scolded me, failed me and mentally torched me for not doing homework or getting low marks in exams. Instead of scolding me, if they tried to analyse the reason for my failure, find my week points and tried to work on it then I would have been a different person by now. But still I love my teachers who at least had a belief in me till last moment that some miracle will happen. But till last day of my academics my teacher and myself waited for the miracle but nothing happened and my teachers lost hope but I am still waiting for the miracle to happen in my life.

Sometimes I used to think, if my science teacher was good to me and instead of giving punishment, mental harassment and making fun of me in front of the class, if my teacher spend a little time in understanding the my issue with leaning science and worked on it then I might have done wonders in science.

Then I would have loved Science and Maths and instead of writing this book, I would have been part of NASA or ISRO and might be using this time to build a plan for the next satellite mission to Mars or Saturn. But god and my teachers were not kind enough to me. They killed the scientist in me at the time when the scientist started taking baby steps inside me. An unintentional murder which no one knows till now. My parents, teachers, friends and my colleagues' and the entire society thinks, I am good for nothing. But no one knows that my purpose of coming to this world has been brutally demolished in my childhood days. No offense to the teaching fraternity, you are the blessed group of people who have been nominated to share light of knowledge to this dark world and take humanity to the next level. But instead of humiliating in front of class for getting low grade, you should analysis the problem in the child. In a class of 30 or 50 students, every one cant be of same calibre.

I believe Teaching should not be merely a job. It should be a passion. A passion to lift a pure and innocent soul with power of knowledge and advice and bring back power with a purpose and goal to face the world. It's identifying the potential and the strength of each student and identifying the weak areas and giving action plans to work on and monitor it on a frequent basis.

So now in ground reality, the world has missed a great scientist ever known to mankind but its okay. A murder of the scientist give birth to a great author. Please don't make fun of this statement, or else you might kill an author too.

So don't Fear the Fear, if you Fear the Fear, Fear will Fear you and if you face the Fear the Fear will flew away. So face the fear and don't run away from fear. Fear is like the Villian of Bollywood movie, from which Hero runs for this entire life. But how ever and where ever he run, by climax of the movie he has the face the villain and is not left with any options.

Identifying Passion or dream in you

Sachin was just an another kid till he got a bat as a gift in his birthday. He was enjoying his childhood days like all other kids at his age. The bat happened to be a turning point in his life. He or his family might never thought that this bat would change his life for ever. The bat was given by somebody but when he got the bat he started gaining interest in cricket and slowly understood his purpose of life and his passion. Slowly the game he started to pass the time becomes his passion and he understand that he is made to play cricket. Then slowly it started taking importance more than any other thing. Day and night his mind can't think anything else than cricket. Then no one had to push him, or wake him in the morning or had to remind him of his goal. His passion worked as a fuel and energy for him and rest is history.

Sachin knows only thing in his life. He only knows to hit the ball with the piece of wood. He doesn't know anything else. He only knows how to hit the ball coming to him at different pace or different swings. For his entire life he just practiced the single skill. But he put his heart and soul to it. he developed his skill to the level that his shots where referred by coming generations and just by seeing the pitch he understand how the wicket behaves and if it's summer what would be the nature of pitch, same pitch in winter how it behaves. Will the pitch suit's the pace bowler or spinner, if it's spinner then leg or off spinner if it's pace which bowler to look for. He knows In an Out of batting. When to be aggressive and when to be defensive. Almost all the shots are there in his book and very rarely makes mistake in batting. That's the level of perfection Sachin has.

so for all of us, all it takes is to find the bat. It's around you, it's in front of you and it's within you. It's somewhat like a treasure hunt, where you have to decode all the clues to find the treasure and mother nature, cosmic energy or god is so kind enough to give clues at every point. But unfortunately 99 % of people fail to understand or decode the clue and 1% will do it neatly by identifying the purpose of life.

God has made everyone with a purpose and some found the purpose or others don't find it for their entire life. There is no written rule on how to do it. but I would say, if you understand yourself then you can some what found the purpose. Talk to yourself on a daily basis, be with yourself and observe on which moment you feel enthusiastic and which moment makes you feel proud and what are tasks you love to do it and what gives the positive vibe to you. Those activities which give a positive vibe should be continued and you will feel the difference. The energy level within you will start increase drastically.

I would again blame our childhood days, where we are free to talk to our self and we had enough time to do it and we were talking to our self, then all the forces in the nature turns against us in the form of parents, teachers our uncles and aunties, siblings and the entire society. We as a child the weakest link the society had no option but to hear. If we rebel then we know the consequences. So our passion and dreams where eaten by academic books and the home works. But it's never too late.

Do what you like, never complaint that you don't have time. We never uses our 24hours for office or professional works. On a daily basis we spend a decent time for not so productive works. All you have to do is, split the time for office and related work and some hours of the day for yourself. Where there is no limitation no restriction no barriers no boarders no boss no tension no frustration and no mask.

You might be wondering, what is the importance of Mask in our life. It is a vital thing in our life. We wear a mask of parent with kid, wear husband mask when we are with our better half , wear mask of a protective family head when we take wife and family for an outing, wear a mask in front of my parents as a obedient son. When I start from home to office I wear a mask of a law bidding citizen who follows all the law of the land and at office a mask of a loyal employee, a mask of a loyal team member and in front client we are like the Bollywood hero who can do anything to make the heroine happy. Here my heroine is my client and I can jump from 10th storied building or I can go to any extent to bring a small pinch of happiness in clients face. Last but not the least, A mask of the minister of the king who always have to bow down to the ruler and forcefully laugh loud on all the creepy or stingy jokes of king and always praises the king when you know he is the biggest (fill the rest by yourself, based on your level of frustration with your boss) . Hope my boss won't read this book or this part of book. If he reads it then I might lose most of the masks and I enjoy everything in life except starving. So better, I stop this point here.

After wearing these much of mask, when will you get time to open all the mask and be yourself. When was the last time you were yourself. We know everything about our friends, kids, wife and everyone close to us. But we don't know much about our self. We only know the habit, likes and dislikes of our self which is not me. My habits are influenced by society and by friends and family. So its obvious that I don't know anything about me. So make friendship with yourself and listen what all I have to tell myself which I desperately wanted to tell, but till now I was not ready or willing to hear me.

So understand the passion or dream in life and never thing that what you are doing currently will justify your talent or potential and if you are not good at it don't think your life is waste.

First thing we must understand. We all are playing a game which we think is the only key way to success and we play sincerely. It's the Game of Comparison. Looks cool. Don't fall in the trap of the game. It's the most dangerous game, which can destroy you completely and it will force you to put down your weapon before the battle starts.

Cactus and Rose can't be compared on it's beauty. Rose has beauty but it can't survive in tough situations. But cactus is not a beautiful plant but it can survive any adverse condition.

If Rose looks at Cactus and starts thinking, Cactus can handle any adverse situation and I can't even handle a strong wind. My life is a waste and there is no point in living a life with limited power and strength and at the same time the Cactus looking at roses and thinking that I am not as beautiful as Rose. Everyone loves roses and no one loves me, then both their life will go on trying to acquire the quality which they are not good at and don't recognize the area where they are good at. So don't compare yourself with others. You are unique creation of god and the skills which you own are also unique.

Don't do a hundred things to prove yourself. Do only one thing that you think you are good at. And practice practice practice till you master it. Then you will be known for the skill. Your time will end one day but the skill you acquire will remain the world till humanity exists. So concentrate on one area and master that.

It take some time, but it's the hope along with hard work keep us going forward.

Dr. Abdul Kalam is not with us now. But we still remember him when ever a rocket takes off from Sriharikota with Indian flag in it. No where in the rocket his name is written and no one takes his name at the time of rocket launch. But we remember him. He didn't try to put his hand and brain in multiple dimensions. His mission was as clear as how mothers loves to her kids. He loved his passion and makes the same as his profession too. I don't think he ever have regretted in his life. Every day he might have enjoyed. Just imagine you are living your dream not for minute or not for some hours for the entire life you are living your dream. How great it can be. Nothing else be more mouth watering that this. So start working on your dreams and search for what is missing in your life and bring it back. The positive vibe you will get will be enough for you to drive the car called life for miles and miles.

Confidence

In my experience, there is a ratio to calculate fear and the ratio is between our confidence and fear. The more the confidence we have the less the fear and more the fear you have less the confidence.

As I mentioned earlier, it's a continuation of fear and confidence, which I think make some relevance in this context. We always should make sure that the level of our confidence should be higher. If it's not, then make your mind believe that you are confident. Convince your mind to the extent that even you are at a situation where you lack confidence, our mind will boost your confidence to the maximum. You can start trying it at home.

The more confidence you have to say to your wife that you forgot to change the diaper of the kid or you forget to wash the dishes or you tell on her face with confidence that you will not clean the house or you will not make breakfast today, the less fear you will have to face the consequence. Jokes apart.

The most leather weapon to suppress fear is the confidence you have to face the situation. I don't have any data to prove my point. Most of you might debate on this point and I can debate on it too without any second thought.

One incident I want to share. I was very introvert by nature. God had played a big prank to me by giving me a job in a company as a Team Leader and where I have to address my team. Have to conduct meetings. In short I have to face all the scary eyes which face me when I speak. (which I feel when I see my team , when I speak) . My heart used to beat fast, sweat and my entire body will be cold , like standing in at Himalayan mountains. For one or two minutes I will be like a person who is paralysed and in a coma and still walking and talking. My brain would be blank and I was seeing heaven and I feel myself as a person who don't know a single step of dance but asked to dance in front of a big audience that also on some sad songs. The situation is like, if I dance. I will die of shame and if I didn't dance, audience will kill me brutally. So left with one option. Select your death and shame is less painful than brutal death and I waiting for the music to start. Everyone in audience laughing at me. Thinking who is this buffalo face monkey who has the mouth of a crocodile and body of a hippo. In short, the feeling is like standing naked in front of the crowd.

I tried to avoid all meetings, send off parties and all the occasions where I need to speak. My lack of confidence is pulling me down and my self-respect is falling at a higher pace than the fall of Nokia's market share. It's reached the bottom. Now no were to go below the level. It reached a level that if I dig a half meter I could have seen oil pumping out of the crust of the earth or I could see the diamonds in the core of earth.

Then I decided. Enough is enough. On a meeting I heard our company's Corporate Training Manger telling that they are looking for Trainers from operations. Then I contacted the Instructor Training Group of our company and I told the manager of the department that I want to be a Trainer. She surprisingly asked, what training you can take. I said, I don't know what I will take. but I want to take some training on facing audience. I want to put myself in a position where, there is no way back and I have to walk through the road. It's quite simple. Do or Die. Die of shame or Die of Pain. But if I came out alive then it would be a paradise and I told her to train me for that and before the session I need a mock session.

She was kind enough to take the risk on me. It was like Biju's app signing Aliya Bhatt to promote their General Knowledge app as their brand ambassador. No offense, it's just a joke. I love her very much for her dedication towards acting.

The instructor had given me enough tips and for the ten days before the session I tried all the possible things to get rid of the only fear of facing audience. Then the judgement day came. I was well prepared. Done all the checks. It was more toughest checks then ISRO or NASA does before launching the rocket. Talked to myself and tried to gain confidence, after sometimes I realized that the bucket where I am filling the confidence has a big hole. I give more confidence to myself and after sometimes I am again nervous. I was searching for the hole, so that I can repair it.

Time was 11:55AM, and at 12:00PM I had to start the session. Audience started entering the hall and they were looking at me and thinking .What is he doing here? Oh might be he changed his department now he might be working in the IT Dept and he might have come to check the laptop and projectors. Some confused and question mark faces I can see. At one moment, I thought of running out of the room screaming by writing a note. "I am going, don't try to find me. by the time you all get this note. I will have reached far away. Tell this to my manager too. Otherwise he will mark Loss of Pay today. Yours Lovingly". It's 12:00PM and the angels around me who were giving confidence, started turning to evil vampire. Sucking my confidence in me and my time starts now. It's Lights Camera and Action.

I revised the Power Point presentation a thousand times and if anyone could have asked me. What is the twentieth word in the tenth slide? I would have told without blinking my eyes. I started with the presentation and went through the slide and completed 20 slides and when I looked at my watch my eyes came out like a big bulls eye. It's only 12:40PM and the session is of three hour long. OH MY GOD.

What, only 40 min out of three hours. What to do next. Verity of thoughts came to my mind. Believe me. Can I tell that your session is over and I give you back two hour and 20 Minute or Can we take a break of 2 hour and then we can have a session of 15 Min or tell them. Till now, I speak you listen now you speak and I will listen. But then the last thought that came to my mind, is to face the situation confidently. Lets see what happen. Drank some water and started to talk. What all comes to my mind I started talking and after fifteen or twenty minutes. My talk started making sense and slowly I got control on what I am saying. I am getting many good points to share and I speak confidently . I am seeing the reaction of the audience changing and I realize that they are listening me. I could start feeling the pumping up of confidence in me. Till that time I was standing near to the laptop at a corner and then slowly I started waking the room and trying to utilize the entire space given to me without intercepting audiences. Words are freely coming from my mind and my hands are not shaking or cold. I am not sweating and everything is normal. My voice is loud and clear and full of confidence. In fact, everything is much much greater than normal.

From that day till now, I enjoyed all my sessions and I love Public speaking. All my fears are gone without leaving a trace.

That day I realised one thing in life. if you try to run from your fear, it will follow you till the end like Private Banks collection agents following the payment defaulters. But if you show some daring. Daring for one or two minute then it's a different game. Choice is ours. Do we have to run our entire life or do we want to face the fear and beat it.

Suicidal act

If you are interested, I can give a tip for free to gain the ultimate confidence in your life. Do you think that you don't have confidence and you can never speak in front of public and do you really want to get rid of the fear without wasting a single penny. Then just do this. I call it Suicidal act. I tried it once, as said above. It will scare you to hell. But after a few minutes, it will regain your confidence and it will give you wings like Red Bull.

Still now I don't understand the tag line of Red Bull, what is the relation between the product name and it's tag line. Bull and Wings. That's so contrary. heavy duty Bull that also Red Bull and tagline of a lightweight bird. Anyways I like it. But it's a little expensive for me. middle class Indian, drink 20 Rs Coke Mini bottle and make sure that not a single drop is left before I throw it. After having kids, I even don't throw it.

I will give to my kid and proudly say, I have brought you a toy. Fill water and play and share it with your brother too. "Say Thanks to Papa".

Coming to the point. Have you ever attended any Training or Town hall session or any other meetings or training where you see a big crowd and in between the presenter is asking. Do you have any questions? The ambience is killing silence. Reminds you of the famous dialogue of Sholey. "Itna Sannata kyun Hai bhai". With a few minutes of pause the speaker continues his presentation.

Now here your role starts. The moment he asks for questions and everyone is waiting for the one person who raises his or her voice.

Without thinking anything or by having a stupid question in mind, just raise your hand. Don't think twice or once. Just raise your hand. Now you are in a situation where the entire crowd is focusing on you and you are in the limelight and every one looks at you with respect till you ask the question. If it's a good question, then after that too. Doors are closed, so you can't ran away from the room and you don't have any other option than to ask anything or at least say anything. Left with two options. You will fall down with Low BP or sudden heart attack or you will face the situation and by going through the one minute, your entire life will be changed. The confidence you get will be immense. If you don't have any questions, just say "I like your session" and sit.

Waiting for the stranger

There are many more reasons why I should do it. First reason is to burst the biggest myth. I don't know about others. But from my school day onwards, if the teacher asks any questions. I will pray to god that someone should answer the question and the question shouldn't come to me. most of the time god was kind enough to save me by coming in one or other form. Some of the studious students answer the question. I don't like that bread of studious students. But that moment I love them more than anything.

Slowly it became my habit. Waiting for the person who can save me from these situations. Whenever God gives me an opportunity I waited for others to take the opportunity. My mind started believing that someone would come and save me from all situations. I waited for the person at every point. My fear also played an important role in giving the opportunity to that person. If I speak what others will think, I will be a point of joke for everyone. Let others take it. I am happy with what I have. Compromised in every situation. My professional career also paid the price for it. My colleagues acted smartly by talking to management and giving ideas and interacting with clients and I thought that I have been saved from all those situations by them.

That someone had taken my chances every time. I wasn't given the chance simply because of my incapability to face the situation. Those who I see as a saviour were actually eating the cake which was meant for me. Then I understand one thing in life. there is no one but me only. If I want to go ahead, I have to take the challenges and I have to face the hardest and bitter moments and more and more I face, the more experience and confidence I will get and believe me, it works.

Now I don't feel ashamed of asking any stupid questions and I don't care who laugh at me. so it's always about you and you only. Don't try to insert another character who can be your saviour. He or she is not your saviour, they are making you handicap in life. your dreams and your happiness should be yours and you have to earn it. Don't wait for your turn. If there is a turn, it should be yours. That's the attitude. If your attitude is strong, then Country like China will also withdraw the troops from the border without putting any demands.

So in short the summary of all these is, key medicine to kill fear is confidence.

Watching flight take off at Airport

One thing which always fascinated me was the Airport and the Aeroplane. I can sit for the entire day in the Airport watching Flight landing and take-off. I am sure many of you might have the same craze like me.

Flight take off teaches us a great lesson, if you watch it carefully. I always got inspired by looking at the sequence from the start. Flight standing at the Airport is like our current situation. Waiting for the push or the spark to start. It's waiting for it's turn. Once the engine is on and slowly taxied from hanger to the runway. That's the moment the instruction is given to it. It slowly starts by it's slow moment, this is the moment when everyone question you passion or talent and want to make you feel low. No one will believe that the machine which weighs 1000 tons has the capacity to fly too. People sitting inside the flight may doubt on it's ability to fly. People standing out and watching it may make fun of it. The flight still moves ahead without giving it's ear to anyone and without doubting it's ability to fly. The moment it doubts it's ability, it will be a scrap and becomes a burden to the airport. A flight which cannot fly is equal to a man who doesn't have a passion and a dream worth chasing for. Flights are not made for land transportation. Same like, I am not made for crawling or walking. God made me to fly high, to catch the highest dreams.

Slowly the flight reaches the edge of it's runway. It will wait at the edge for some minutes. Looking at the runway. It's not the break which it is taking for relaxing. That's the minutes when the flight is seeing nothing in front of it. The flight is just seeing the blue sky and clouds. Its only seeing its dream of flying is just minutes away. It prepare itself. Realizes that the distance between it and his dreams is very less. it sees it's dream to fly is only a few feet away. It knows the power and speed it requires. It knows in seconds, it has to reach a speed of 240 to 280Kms per hour to fly. Seems difficult, but worth a try. It wait's and then it gathers all it's energy to a single point as the plane knows, it don't have a drop of energy or time to waste and to fly it require the full energy it has. So for next two minutes, noting on it's mind. Only the blue sky and the required power to reach there. Even minute power of the reading lamps inside the flight will be routed towards the engine to boost it's power. Now it's do or die. with a roar it moves ahead. No doubt on it's mind. It puts all it's efforts. The last drop of blood and sweat is dropped for a single aim. To reach the speed. No thoughts, nothing else in mind. It suffers all the pain and wounds it gets in the process. But doesn't lower it's speed and finally when the speed is achieved.

When the speed is achieved then just a flip of a wing and the thousand ton of metal started flying in air with out any support. A moment worth of millions. Now the flight might be living it's dream. A dream to fly.

When everyone doubted its flying capability, it was not listing to the critics and getting depressed. It was working hard on all the possible way to reach the max spread on runway.

What if the flight which was standing at the edge of the runway got frightened by the runway and returned back to the hangar?

What if the flight came at the edge of the runway and you may hear many comments. You can't fly. When train, bus or cars don't fly. So how can you fly. who are you to fly. You can never fly. How dare you to fly. You are a failure. You fatty boy, With these 1000 tons of weight. You think you can fly. You are loser and don't dream big, you are good for nothing, burden to parents, society and to the world, you are the biggest loser and many more comments.

That's life and many of us have sacrificed many dreams due to these negative comments. The most deadly words which can paralyze our dreams is "What others will think" and "you cant do it, it's not your cup of tea".

If you live for others, you will find yourself in the hanger for your entire life, but if you believe in yourself. You will put all your energy to fly high.

You can't always fight and close mouth of those who have doubted on it. You can't debate with them and win it. Instead of that, prove yourself. So that no one will dare to question you. choice is yours.

Choice is simple from two options. What I think about me and what others think about me. Which statement is more important in your life will decide your future.

Filter Machine

I developed a new gadget for myself and for me it's the greatest invention . As part of the disciplined and very much social society. I didn't run naked from my bathroom after inventing the gadget by shouting Eureka.

The invention that I done for myself is a filter machine. Which can filter the comments from the society and everyone who is near to me. The main highlight of the machine is that, it will mute some words before it touches my ear drum and goes to my brain. Words like "Can't do it, you are a looser, enjoy for some more time, don't work, goussips etc". Instead of accepting the comments blindly. Now I started to filter . Do I have to react to the situation or can I leave it. Do I have to keep this in my mind or can I ignore it? Do I have to carry the comment and change my behaviour towards the author of the comment or the father of the comment. Is there anything for me to change or is it like the manifesto made by the political party? Which has no value after the election is over.

Think and act. Life is not that complicated as we make it or think it is. It's quite simple.

It's all about the data we accumulate in our brain. It's the information from our past experience which the brain analyses and provides the decision on any situation. If the data that we input in our brain has a negative vibe to it, then definitely the brain throws negative vibes in all our thinking and decision making. If any teenager makes fun of you or any college student gang tries to bully you. it doesn't mean that entire teenagers or college students are disrespectful towards elders. But the data we feed to the brain like all teenage and college students are bullies and youth is disrespectful then our life would be more miserable when some of these groups of people look at us or smile at us or try to come forward for a decent friendship. Our brain will not accept the later part as the input is already given to it and the input given to the brain is a password protected file. You can access it, view it but you can't change anything in it.

So it would be a good practice to think about a situation before making a decision. My brain should react as per the information I give to it. Which has a logical reasoning. Not to take a situation as it is. All the situations should be properly dissected and should undergo a proper post-mortem and understand the situation from different perspectives and see the same situation from different points of view and multiple dimensions should be taken into consideration before you give any input to the brain .

You might be laughing at this methodology and might have the question, who in this world has this much time?

But I would say, the input which you give to your brain and which holds the power to change my perception tomorrow should be worth investing some time today to build a better version of me for tomorrow. I believe the way we handle situations makes a big difference. Some people try to see what the world shows them and some people try to see what's hiding behind the scene which is the truth but it's not seen in the first instance. So instead of regretting later on a decision you have taken by jumping the guns, it's always good to analyse and make a wise decision.

There was a beautiful and heart touching story I read sometimes back. Of Course on Social media. Like you all, I too believe that reading a story in a book or reading an article from paper is time consuming. Hear the news online and scroll on social media, which is the trend nowadays.

There was a small kid who had done some scratches in his dad's new car and his dad got so angry with the kid that he beat the kid without mercy and finally the kid lost his fingers and later when the dad came near to the car. The kid has written "I love you Dad so much" and his dad can't forgive himself for what he had done to his kid.

I hope you all got the morale of the story. So have patience in life. It pays well at times. One good thing my life teaches me is to wait, think and act. Not the otherwise Act, think and regret. Change the sequence and it will bring wonders to your life.

I would prefer to be a Rahul Dravid who takes his time to study the pitch and study the bowler and the conditions of the terrain and the intensity of sledging in the field and all analysis all other factor before coming up with a plan rather than Virandra Shawag who knows only one thing with bat. To play shots, whatever the situation. But on a long run, players like Rahul Dravid survive . He might be criticized for his less aggressiveness and less use of reflex actions. But in the long run these are the players who write history.

The best example is the Army. When there is an emergency or a war. The Army will only send those troops first who know the conditions well and understand the tactics and strategies which can be executed on that terrain and the troops who can survive and execute plans in the zone.

So all it takes is to understand the situation and execute plans based on the situation.

Opportunities

Some time I used to think, why god is kind to some people and unkind to many. As I told earlier, the bat Sachin got in his childhood days brings his passion towards cricket. What if he didn't get that bat or the Goal keeping capability of MS Dhoni not seen by his coach. What if Mark Sukemburg, Bill Gates and Steve Jobs didn't drop out of college? So it's like God had shown them their path by putting a situation in front of them and it's really unfair that the same god didn't give me a bat at my birthday and there was no coach to see my talent in the field and unfortunately I was not a dropout from college. "Why not me... god".

Then I realise, I might have lost many opportunities that might have come to me, but I didn't realise it as an opportunity. When I start thinking a little deeper on this topic I understand one thing. To be successful in life, we should first understand our limit's. Now I don't know my limit. Unless I run a marathon how can I know what my stamina is? Am I a product of a 5km marathon or 10 km or straight 20 km.

I have a very bitter but now a beautiful experience of my first marathon. It was two years back I think. To be precise 2 years BC. Don't get me wrong. I am not a person who by mistake reached this planet through time travel. I mean 2 Years Before Covid.

I happened to see a advertisement in FB regarding a Marathon and those where the time I started to go to Gym and do some thread mill. I managed to complete 2 KM in 10 to 15 min over thread mill and it gives confidence that I can compete in any marathon. My mistake. It gives me an over confidence. On the site of registration I was asked to choose the Km. it was having 5km and 10km. I asked myself, can I choose 5km. immediately my brain replied. Bro you are not a material for 5km. it's for kid. You are born to do much more than that. Go for 10 + km. I thought, it's my first attempt, 10km will be enough for a try. I see that as an opportunity to prove my stamina and power as an athletic. I collected by kit and I ordered Bluetooth earphones and some other items. The day came and I started from home at 5:00AM. Told my wife "Baby you sleep, today world is going to see a rise of a star. Your will see the Tarzan in me". With full energy I reached. I was fully equipped with everything possible I need. Have a hand pouch for my mobile. Sweatband and what all possible. Most of the people were looking at me. thinking that I am a professional . then time for some warm up Zumba. I was like, don't waste my time. I want to show the world who I am. Then the flag off. I was so excited, I started running slowly and with in five min I was tired and I can't breathe and I can't walk also. I can see that small kids and old retired people are overtaking me and I was not running, not walking literally scrolling and due to shame I removed my ear phone and removed all the fancy items which was endorsing me as professional runner and kept in pocket and started walking as if, I am going to buy milk and bread and I don't know what is happening here. When I see, no one was watching me. I start running then within one or two min my energy will be exhausted and back to walk. When I reached the halfway point, I can count the stars and birds flying around my head and I was going to hallucination. I started seeing my grandparents in front of me and they were angry with me for spoiling the name of the family and I can see the beautiful angels who were laughing at me and murmuring.

See, this is the guy who came to be a star and now he is like a five year old Christmas star hanging in the branch of mango tree which is only used by birds to do shit. But then I realized the most shocking truth which shocked my body and soul to the extent that my soul was planning to go out without any notification or notice period .

You know, what was that truth? From the halfway mark, I have to go back 5km for my car. Somehow I managed to complete the marathon. Don't ask me how. But I completed it. If you still don't trust me, I have put the photos on FB. Go and check and you will realise that Vijay never lies.

When I was coming back from Marathon, I was thinking that till now I was living in a fool's paradise and now I realise I can't even run 100 meters at a single stretch on ground.

From that date, I started participating in almost all the marathons and improved my capacity. Now I can run nearly 8.6km in a hour. I know it's not good timing. But for me taking time from my schedule and doing this much. It's a wow factor for me. My motivation started when I was able to run 1km in a stretch.

So now my point is, if I didn't understand my limitation. I wouldn't be motivated to improve. Whenever I run a single meter extra than my previous run, it's the motivation for me to try for the next meter extra run for tomorrow.

Understanding the finishing line is the starting line of your game. You should first understand your finishing line and then improve it on a daily basis.

On my childhood days, I heard a story. The meaning of the story, I understood lately.

There was a church in a village and the church had a priest who dedicated his life to serve god. He did everything good. Helped people, didn't care for his health. Always ready to help anyone who comes to him. He didn't marry, thinking that his devotion towards god will reduce and he has to share his love to his wife and to god.

On a day, the village was very badly hit by a flood. Water level was rising slowly and a rescue team came with a boat and rescued the villagers and the priest was standing on the roof of the church. One rescue boat came and people inside the boat shouted. Father came to the boat, we came to rescue you. Priest says, you can go. God will come and rescue me. the second boat came and his answer was the same and the third boat came just for the priest and the answer was the same and slowly the water level rose and the priest drowned in the water and he died.

When the priest opened his eyes, he realised that he is in heaven in the hands of god. But the priest doesn't seem to be happy. God asked him. What happened my son, you are not happy to meet me.

Priest said sadly. I dedicated my entire life serving you. I do whatever possible to make you happy. I only lived as per your instructions and I thought when I had a problem, you would come and help me. When I was drowning I called you several times. But you never responded.

God smiled and told. I had sent three boats for you and the third boat I sent only for you. You didn't get into the boat. How can you blame me for it.

Morale of the story, we are waiting for god to come and give us what all we need. We don't realise the opportunity which he had given by god.

God says, you put your whole hearted effort and I will do the rest. Without doing anything from our part we used to pray to god to give this give that and in one minute of praying, it's a four to five page of wishes and favour we ask to god. Some times when I stand in front of god and started to open my wish list, I feel like myself as a beggar who only knows begging and don't know anything else. Just asking for one or another thing which even I am not eligible to get it.

God has already given us every thing we require. A perfect working body and a perfectly thinking mind and perfect vision and a perfect platform. Now why we have to beg or ask for anything more. He had given us what we want. Just make full use of it and then stand in front of him with full of positivity and full of confidence by believing that I have done my part. Now it's your turn. If you can shower your blessings on my hard work then it would be great. Otherwise also no problem, I still have a perfect body , perfectly thinking mind and perfect vision. I can try once again. that's how we should move ahead in life.

Expectations

We all have much expectations from life. Expectations are like the immortal beings, which you won't be able to kill. The more you kill expectation the more it will rise. The more you fulfil your Expectations the more bigger it will become and come back to you. So expectations are not some thing which we can ignore or avoid so easily. but one thing is there, when an expectation is completed then it will give a good pump of happiness in our life. But unfortunately for only a small time.

Expectation of getting promotion is fulfilled for a day or a week and then the expectation will be some thing more. Even US President might have a bigger expectation from his life. The problem with the expectations is that, when it's not fulfilled then it will add negativity to your life. If expectations are satisfied then we enjoy . So always work hard and smart with a dream not with an expectations because all the that you do today, it's not necessary that it will pay off by tomorrow. For some work you will get the payment or appreciation on the same day but for some other work the appreciation or payment will take days months or years to come by. If you do all the work expecting a result soon then within a week or so, you will quit the work and god knows you might be an outstanding person doing that work, but just because you didn't get the appreciation you left the work. You have killed a hero or an achiever in you before it's even born. So do all the work with passion and with full dedication and with whole heart but not with expectation.

You can have the expectation , but don't fix a time line to the expectation. Let the appreciation or payment takes it time to come to you. You continue doing what you were doing and do the best.

There was a beautiful story in Hindu Mythology , one day a friend of Sree Krishna named Kuchala decide to visit to Krishna. Kuchalan was Kirshnan's childhood friend and after a long time he is going to see Krishna. That also his wife forced him to see Krishna . As their Financial situation was not good and it's getting worse day by day. So Kuchala's wife asked him to go and meet Krishna and tell his current situation , so that Krishna will do some help as Krishna is the king of Dwaraka.

So he started the journey toward Dwaraka. he was carrying a small bag of flattened rice as a gift to his childhood friend. But he was afraid whether it's a good gift to present to a king. But he don't have any other option. At his current position he doesn't have anything else to give to the king. He is actually not willing even to go to meet Krishna but his wife insisted him to go and tell his current situation to the king.

So after the long journey he reached Dwaraka and managed to get appointment get in the royal hall where King Krishna meet everyone. He even doubted, if Krishna would even recognised him or not. To his wonder, Krishna came running towards him and hugged him and told. It take so long for you to come and meet me and by hearing that Kuchana's eyes were wet that the biggest king of the era recognised him and came to him and hugged him which he never thought would ever happen. Krishna asked Kuchala, " haven't you brought anything for me". Kuchala was hesitating to give the bag o flattened rice to Krishna as he can see the royal place and there are many chefs who are making delicious and mouth-watering food for the king and he wondered, if Krisna would ever eat his below ordinary flattened rice. But with half mind, he gives the bag to Krishna and like a small hungry boy Krishna eat all the flatten rice and with smiling face he told. This is the best food I have ever ate in my life which makes Kuchala cry.

Krishna insisted him for staying with him for four to five days and on all these days he thought of telling Krishna about his financial position but he was not able to tell him, because all these time he was thinking that. What Krishna will think. After these long time, his friend came to meet him and that also to ask for financial help. The day has come when he had to go back to his home and on that day also he was not able to tell about his position but he was not sad. He was very much happy with the way Krishna treated him. Kuchala thought, it's not a good idea to ask any favour. Let me leave my situation to mine to god and he started traveling back towards his village. When he reached his home, he was surprised to see a beautiful house and his wife and children were wearing expensive dresses and ornaments and his kitchen is filled up with delicious foods and every one was so happy. It take a while for Kuchala to realise, if it's a dream or what. When he asked his wife, what happened here. His wife handed him a letter. It was the letter from Krishna which mentioned that " a return gift for the most delicious bag of flattened rice".

Suppose, if Kuchala was expecting much from Krishna the biggest ruler of his time and didn't get what he has expected. Then definitely, he will be disappointed with his old friend. Now he didn't expect anything from his friend and what all he get back makes him more than happy. Even if he didn't get any help from Krishna then also he would be happy. Even if his friend didn't recognise him after a long then also he would be happy.

Even if his friend didn't eat the flattened rice then also he would be happy. Even if his friend didn't send any financial help or other sort of help then also he would be happy.

Expectations are directly tagged with many conditions. These conditions have the capacity to change our emotions or our mind set. Conditions are, if things works above expectations then the condition is more than happy. If things works up to expectations the condition is happy and if things didn't worked as expected then condition is not happy, sad, disappointed, frustrated, irritated etc. Suppose, If I am not tagging any conditions to my expectation and my expectation is free from all conditions then how the situation will be. If my expectation is fulfilled I am happy, if my expectation is half fulfilled then also I am happy, if my expectation is below half fulfilled then also I am happy even if my expectation is not fulfilled then also I am not sad but happy.

Too much expectation from life makes us more nervous and it can lead to depression or any psychological issues too where the gravity of the effect to our mind, brain and towards the body will be more than expected.

Just want to share one more story which I have seen some where, but it touches my heart.

There was a small boy, who was very much hungry and going shops to shops begging for food. No one bothers to give anything and more than that some peoples pushes him and shouted at him. There was a street vendor who was selling bread and milk. She called the boy and gives him bread and her daughter gives him milk to drink. After having the milk and bread, the boy looks at her and told. Now I don't have any money to pay to you but I owe you the bread and milk for my entire life and he ran away crying.

Time passes away and this lady was old now she is admitted to hospital due to a major heart attack and her daughter was stating outside the operation theatre praying to god for her mother's health and she don't know how to settle the big bill of operation. Doctor came and told her, not to worry. Your mother is out of danger. She was very much tension free now but the operation and hospital bill. She asked the Doctor, how much is the bill for the operation. Doctor smiled and told her. You can go to the accounts department and check. With a blank mind she went to the accounts department and asked for bill. Her hands were shivering as she knows that she will be going to get the biggest shock of her life. After waiting for five minute one person came with a bill which was in a envelop. With all the courage and left energy she opened the bill and prayed to all god. She noticed a note on the Bill which says "Bill paid against one full glass of milk and bread". She didn't understand what does that mean. She asked the accounts team and they confirm that the bill has been cleared for operation and hospital charges and even for the upcoming regular hospital visit's and you don't have to pay anything. With confused face she was standing in the hospital and later she came to know that the doctor who had done the operation is the same boy which her mother called and given the milk and the bread.

An act of humanity without expecting any return will be repaid by any form when you need the most. It's a universal truth. As said by Issac Newton, "Every action has an equal and opposite reaction". Do your action now with full of passion and dedication and don't expect the result. There is no way that you have done an action and you didn't get the reaction of it. In Hindu religion it's called Karma. Karma is a universal fact. you will get the fruit of the seed which you bowed .

Many of us feel that, there is no fun in doing things without any expectation. Expectation is the motivational factor for performing any tasks or activities. It would like going on a drive without knowing the destination. But I have a different opinion to it.

The excitement should be there on the action. The fun factor should be there on the task or action that you do, not on the final product. It's same like, having a long drive to an exotic place with your wife and the road is very much bumpy and full of pit's, half the road is damaged and you are struggling to drive the whole way. You are taking all the pain to reach to the destination. When you reached the destination, do you think you have enough energy left with you to really enjoy the destination. Three forth of your energy is already drained out and you have left with only one forth energy which can only take you to bed. Suppose, if the road is smooth and it's a big high way with very less traffic and the weather is so romantic and you are driving the same car with of course with your same wife and you are enjoying each and every moment of the drive and when you reach the destination then you the energy level will be double when compared to the earlier scenario and you will enjoy that moment to full extent and even if the destination is not as good as you expected then also you won't feel disappointed as you have enjoyed most of your day on the drive.

So the drive is important than the destination. So enjoy what you are doing so that, if the result is not up to the mark but still you can be satisfied with the effort you put. It's always said " Do what you like or Love what you do ". the option is with us. If you got an opportunity to do what you like then you are among the few lucky peoples in the planet who had got the opportunity like this. Enjoy the way and the destination.

For the second one, if you are not so fortunate and have to select a profession which you don't like, but you are not left with any option other than to select the work as a mean to earn bread and butter to the family. In that case, instead of cursing you and all those who have put you to this situation. If we can start loving what we do. It would be like the girl next door who doesn't look pretty when compared to the other girls who spend much time in beauty parlour or spend a good amount of money on dressing. In front of all those beauties the girl living in next door seems to be out dated. But, if you ignore all the other girls in the colony or your town and just see her when ever it's possible. I can guarantee you that , after a point she would like a Miss Universe or Miss World and you don't feel like seeing other girls. When she smile, you will be filled with positive energy and when she talks, you just want to hear sweet voice and you will be addicted to her. Hopefully my wife can understand, this is just an example I am sharing. Otherwise her expectation towards me will change completely and my reality and expectation will be messed up.

So my point is, if you think your work is boring and there is no excitement in it. Then you have change your mind set. Start enjoying each activities you do at your work place and don't peep into others cabin. Just you and your work. Then after some time you will start enjoying your work. Try to find out the excitement factor in your work. Every work has an excitement factor. It's our vision and our current mind set which is not finding it.

So from now onwards, find the Miss Universe in your work place and enjoy your work. Majority of our time in a day we are spending for work and suppose, if we are not happy with that work. Literally it means, you are killing yourself on a daily basis and if it continues for years then it would be a worthless life in this beautiful planet.

Vision in life

Another important aspect in life is the Vision. It's an area which cannot be ignored when put in the context of improving yourself. No one in the entire world hasn't tasted success without having a vision in life. A Vision should be set before starting to chase a goal.

I will start with a small story from my life. Me and two of my friends happened to go for a holiday trip to Manali. One of the beautiful places to visit in North India. There we planned to visit Rohtang pass. It's a breath taking experience to visit that place. I would strongly recommend everyone to visit that place once in a life time. It's around 13,000 feet from sea level and on that point you feel a little difficulty in breathing. If you are person who spend most of the time sitting in front of the system and don't do any physical exercise. Then you might feel the hardness.

When we reached Rohtang Pass, the weather was good. Which we feel by looking outside from car where all the windows were closed and A/C was kept on mild cooling, it's as equal to off mode. Sun was there without showering much of his light, but partially blessing the mountains with his light. When we get out of the car, we realise that Sun doesn't have a role there. Even the Sun light was there, it was too cold. we were shivering and we see one local guy was selling tea and never before the hot tea tasted so much without much tea dust and sugar. But it was the only option to get rid of the cold and we started taking photos as all tourists do. Then slowly we walked towards a mountain where the view was very nice and I see a hill on another direction and noticed that the hill is blocking a view of a breath taking view of the valley underneath and huge mountains on the other side. Snow covered mountains and valleys and small lakes. I told my friends that we can climb that hill and on the top of the hill we will get some extra ordinary view. But me and my friends are shivering and having little difficulty in breathing also. My friends straight away rejected the proposal and told the climb is too hard and here itself we are facing hard time breathing and it's too cold here, there the situation will be more worse and climbing would need a good inhale and exhale of air and now our lungs are overloaded. I watched the hill for some time and thought of giving a try. It's a life time offer. You came up to here and going without seeing the view is not fair. It might remain in my mind for ever. After a long time, the thought might haunt me. As I was so near to the breath taking view and just because of some silly reason I didn't climb it. After a long debate between me and myself, I won and I told my friends that I am going to the hill and request them to wait for at least half an hour.

Started my climb, it was very difficult for five to ten minute. The climb was little difficult, not as easy as it look from far. I was little bit afraid too. It was me only climbing the hill and if I fall or if something happen to me there won't be any one to help me. But me and the silence around the hill and the sound of the blowing wind started talking to each other and after some time, I started enjoying the climb and at last reached the top and believe me, I swear. I was speechless to see the amazing view from the top of the hill. Truly a miracle by god and I don't have any words to describe it. I stand there speechless for some time and as a tourist taken some photos. As I was a good photographer, which I later realised is a false statement, when I see the photos taken from the hill, after I landed down from the hill. The worse photo one can take of such an exotic view. Till now, I used to think that the one of the best decision I made in my life is to climb that hill and still the fifteen or twenty minute I spend on the top of the hill is as fresh memory as what I eat today in breakfast.

Then I realised one thing, it the vision which makes the difference in life. Me and my friends were standing and watching the same hill from same angle and under same sun light. When I asked them to come with me, they were seeing the height of the hill and difficulty in climbing the hill and difficulty in breathing and the born chilling cold to bring up to the conclusion that it's really a bad idea or plan to climb the hill. But with the same view and with the same angle and under the same sun light I was seeing the view beyond the hill. The curious child was active in me and the child was so active that he was engulfing the height of the hill and difficulty in climbing the hill and difficulty in breathing and the born chilling cold. I could not feel these as an obstacle for not climbing the hill. I was not able to see anything else than the other side of the hill and they were not able to see anything else than the obstacles.

That's my point. We all will have different opinion about the same situation and it's about how we look at the situation. If you look everything negative about the situation then you will never ever face the situation and come out of it but if you see the situation as an opportunity then it's a different story. It's all about how you look at the hill. if you look at climbing the hill as an act of tiredness or painful then for the entire life you will be standing at the ground and watching the hill and after some time you will start blaming everyone for not allowing you to climb, not motivating you or your responsibilities or liabilities pulled you back or lack of time which didn't allowed you to climb up the hill. Whatever is the reason. In your mind you know, that you are consoling yourself for the missed golden opportunity, but you don't want to accept the fact that it's your mistake or it's your call for not climbing the hill. At last when you identify that it was an opportunity then it would be really late and you don't have any other option than to regret for not grabbing the opportunity. Believe me regret is one of the most painful emotion which can lead the frustration and depression and to live a life with regret is like carrying a ton of steel on the head for most part of your life. The thought like "If I could have done that, or if I could have taken the opportunity or if I could have said yes" then my life would be entirely different.

When you have a vision in life, it should be crystal clear and don't doubt about it and don't doubt on your ability or competencies to complete the task. If you doubt about your goal or vision then you will have a second thought that do I have to jump to it or am I wasting my time and energy.

There is a beautiful story in Mahabharata, where the Pandavas and Kauravas where learning Archery. There Master Drawnacharya asked everyone who was aiming a dummy bird eye which was kept in a mango tree with the bow and arrow. He came to everyone and asked. What can you see? Some of his student told that they can see the leafs some told that they can see bird mangoes behind the bird and some told that they can see the entire tree. When the Master asked Arjun. Arjun told that he can only see the eye of the bird. His Master again asked him, can you see the mangoes on the tree. Arjun said No. Master again asked, can you see the leafs. Arjun again told No. Master again asked "can you see the branches" again the same answer "No". Arjun told. Sorry Master, I don't see the mangoes, leafs or branches. I can only see the eye of the bird apart from that eye

I can't see anything else and later on history remembers him as the greatest Archer ever lived in earth. That's how the Vision should be. When you see a dream and you are setting the same dream as your goal of life and forming a vision then first thing is that, you should only see the goal. Nothing else there can be mangoes leafs or branches in between. The moment you start noticing these mangoes, leafs or branches or the entire mango tree then the chances of achieving your dream will be reducing. The more concentrated you towards your dream the more you can get close to it.

I believe there is a difference between a Vision and a Goal. A Vision is set for a long term. It's a big dream which can transform your life and your image entirely. But to get there you have to cross so many huddles. That's the Goals or AIM. A Vision is structured with lots of goals and AIM. These Goals and AIMs are like milestone on the way which will make you realise that you have climbed a step and getting a step closer towards the dream. It not about seeing the long path and getting disappointed by thinking that I have completed only one step now. It about believes that I have completed one step and only 99 more to go. Isn't that a positive thought?

Have you ever thought of the difference between a Goal and a Vision? When we were studying in School and at the end of the year we all have a Goal, which is to pass the exam and try to score as much marks and we put our best of the best effort for it. The two or one month before the exam we will sacrifice everything which was so near and dear to us. Social Media, Friends and all those things which usually keep us motivated to live a pleasant life and all our energy and effort will be put for a single Goal. That is to pass the exam. But the moment the exam is over the set goal is completed and only after one year there will be a second goal on the form of next exam. In between there is no goal. We live an ordinary life with all the enjoyment in life and without any goal.

But instead of Goal, just imagine you have a vision in your mind. To be a Doctor, Pilot or to be an IIT'n from a reputed university or a Pilot etc. Then you will understand these exams are not the final point of Goal. It's just a mile stone which need to be crossed to enter the next level and the next level is not the end of game. There are lot of huddles in the way and our mind won't consider this as a final goal and once one goal is achieved then second goal and third goal.

Even our mind had a problem with Goal. How many of you people remember the name of subjects which you studied in your last year of academics. Not all, just try to remember three to four without a putting pressure on brain. Have you ever realised that once the exam is over then after a couple of days we started forgetting what we have learned and after one month, we forget most of the potion which we studied by waking up early in the morning or by sitting late night. We tend to forget each and every thing slowly which we have learned by taking so much effort. It's because we have given clear instruction to our mind that the goal (which is getting good marks or passing the exam) is the end point of the mission and when our mind realise that the goal is completed it will slowly delete all that is learned or all the efforts which we have taken to achieve it. It will clear the memory and keep it reserve for the new information.

When it comes to Vision, it won't stop at any goal. If the Vision is set then the Goals won't be an important aspect for our mind. It will only consider Goals as a part and parcel of the vision.

Focus on the vision and work for it, to achieve the vision set goals and monitor its status frequently. Never ever get satisfied or quit vision when you achieve the goal. Most of us tend to do this mistake. Like once the Goal is achieved we decide to take a break and later start the next phase. But these breaks will let down the fire in you slowly it will make you move out of the track. Always remember, it's a comparatively easy task to set a vision but it's very difficult task to put in on daily routine and follow it religiously and if the second part is not taken care then it's the end of Vision and Goal.

So concentrate on your short term, medium term and long term goal by keeping in mind that it's a road map to my big dream. Take small small steps. Even if it's a baby step, a step is a step and you have all the right to celebrate the completion of every single step. Without these small steps your life will be stagnant and will be covered with fungus and rust.

Failures in Life

We always consider Failure as a bad spirit or a bad evil or a monster who wants to take away all the happiness from our life. We always try run away from the monster call failure. But we tend to forget one thing that we learned in our initial stage of life. When we were a small baby. After falling many times we all started walking confidently in our life and all the things where we have a learned a new skill is by falling or failing many times.

I want to share my experience. Many years back, I was working in Dubai and I have registered for Driving licence and those who don't know about the getting a Driving license in Dubai , I would like to say. It's not easy to get the licence in United Arab Emirates. You need to sweet out to the core to get a driving licence. A small mistake made at the driving test and you are fail even if you didn't commit any mistake then also to pass in the Driving test depends upon the mood of the Inspector who monitor our driving skills.

At that time, I was working on a small company and my salary was even smaller when compared to the scale of the company. Total expenses for the Driving licence are much higher when I compared the expense with my salary and in short I have taken a big risk.

Taken the risk and taken money from everywhere possible I can get money. But by Grace of good God, things where much different than my expectation and I failed on four driving tests and lost all the hope and I can see my dream of getting Driving licence shattering in front of me like a Castle of cards and I was just able to see it silently. I can see the hole in my ship and I can only watch my ship sinking in front of me and my hands and body are tied with the financial burden and mind is blocked from making any decisions and I was watching my ship sinking in the water and it was pitch dark in front of me and I know that I should better quit as I know, now it's only ship is sinking and if I didn't quit now. I will sink in financial debts and won't be able to get out of it with that salary.

But one of my friend, who was more like my mentor to me asked me just to give one more try and if you didn't passed on that too then leave it. He told not to quit easily when you have come this far. After sometimes I make up my mind to give a last try and join for one week of Driving class before the test and I was assigned a Driving instructor who was very rude and don't have any mercy. Driving class was of one hour and that one hour sitting in the car near to the instructor was like sitting in a torcher chamber where you don't know what is the next tool that is used to torcher me. Don't know when my torcher starts will. But one thing is for sure. I will not be spared at any cost. He used to beat me on my thighs so hard, if I make any mistake and really it hurt badly and when I say, it's bad. it's really bad. Sometimes I can count stars flouting in front of my eyes and by the end of the my driving I don't feel the pain any more as my thigh lost sensations and I was still going for the one hour driving class as it was my last ray of hope. So without complain I completed it for one week and this one week my instructor never talked to me or even smiled at me a single time. He opened his mouth to give instructions and to shout at me.

I used to curse him to the extent that if my curse work then hell would be a small place for him and hell don't have these much things which was on my curse and some time I used to cry silently in the car with pain but I never shown it my face. Controlled all my emotions and it was only the tears which will roll from my eyes which I was not able to control. All my frustration I used to take on the steering wheels.

After one week of training completed and I get out of the car by saying Thanks to the instructor and started walking and I hear a soft voice from my back. It was my instructor, he was calling me and I walked to him and asked him. Yes Sir. To my biggest surprise of my life, I seen that guy smiling at me and he patted me on my shoulder and asked me tomorrow 1:30PM is your test, right?. I replied "Yes" and he told me that this test you will pass for sure. You have good confidence now and you are driving well. The next thing what he told me again bring tears on my eye. Not the tears of pain. He told me "I have beaten you very hard many a times in this one week and I was so harsh with you, it's only to improve your driving skills. If I was soft to you, you will repeat the mistakes again and again. But now when you even think of committing a mistake consciously or unconsciously, the thought of the pain of my beating will never allow you to make the mistake. Now at no point of your driving you will commit any mistake because for all the possible mistakes you can make I have given you enough pain to remember for rest of your life and you won't repeat it again. So now you are a perfect driver for UAE road. I have made you drive in all the roads in this one week. From highway to pocket roads and made you face the entire possible situation one can face in driving in UAE. Tomorrow confidently drive the car and you will surely get the driving license. He hugged me and softly said "Sorry, don't take me wrong". Next day as he said, I gone for the driving test and that without any tension I attempted the test and I passed.

Believe me, from that day till now. It's been more than 12 to 13 years, I drive many cars and Pick up vehicles up to 3 ton and haven't done a single accident and till now I didn't even allowed to make a small scratch also to any vehicle I drove on road. I was and I am always alert once I sit in the driving seat. I remember my instructor as a villain who came to my life for one week but till now I remember each and every lesson he taught me. The lessons I learned with pain.

Some time I used to think that, if I have passed on my first attempt or second or if I didn't get the hard core training from my instructor then I would been an ordinary driver. Might be the worst driver you can ever see on a road. But just because I failed on my first four attempts and got the strictest instructor I have become a good driver.

So failure is not the end of the story or end of life. It stores some most valuable lessons which we you will cherish later in life. The dead end which we find at the point of failure is a new starting to a different world. The darkness of the failure is not the darkness of Graveyard it's the darkness just before the sunrise.

Failure teaches us some great lesson and makes us a venerable asset which world will look for in the future. The more failure and hard time we have to face the more our confidence and potential will rise. Life and career goes to an uptrend when it has more and more obstacles and bumpy way. Failures will bring the best version of you in future.

But if you run from the failure, then the trace of failure will follow you were ever you go and to the last day of your life the failure will attack you and will not leave any inch land for you to hide. But if you dare to face the failure it will give more and more ways and open many paths for you to succeed which you have never dreamed off.

It reminds me a story which I have heard some times back. There was a farmer who loves his crops and plants so much but he was not happy with the rain and strong winds which his plants and crops has to face in its life time. Once he asked god not to give heavy rainfall or heavy wind to his farm as he don't like to see his plants and crops struggle and fight with these rain and heavy wind to be alive and God was kind enough to hear his wish and god granted the wish which makes him jump with joy.

He daily watered his plants and crops and was happy to see his plants are growing at good pace and as promised by god, there was no heavy rain and strong winds which came that year to touch his plants and crops and days passed by and now it's the time to harvest and he was happy and expecting a good harvest on the season, as he believed that his plants and crops will give him the best harvest of his life time as this season there was no heavy rain or heavy wind.

He walked to his farm and to his surprise there was no fruit's or grains in any of the plants. These plants and crops had grown to the height as expected but not a single fruit or gain is there. He was confused and devastated to see the scene and finally decided to ask God the reason for this.

He asked to God, "God, I have done everything possible for my plants, I have taken care of these corps with great love and passion and give all the fertilisers to them to grow at good pace and this year, I myself watered the entire farm as there was no heavy rain for me as per my wish and why there is not a single fruit or grains in my plants".

God replied " It's true that you have done everything possible which you can do for your plants and crops, it's you who have given them the good food which they need, it's you who have removed all the bugs which can affect the plants, it's you who have given the water to them, it's you who have removed all the dried leaves, it's you who had made sure that birds and other animals doesn't destroy your crops, it's you who have taken all the possible steps to make your plants and crops grow at good pace, it was you who had given all the comfort to your plants and protect it from every situation and it was you who have pampered your crops to the extent that they are very much depended on you but it was me who used to give the heavy wind and heavy rain which has the power to throw the plants and crops from its root and for the same reason the plants and crops to protect itself from the heavy winds and rain it will work hard to deepen their roots in the soil and prepare itself for the next wind and rain, it was me who have thought them how to handle the adverse situation and when they put their roots deep inside the soil the more strength they will get and more productive these plants and crop will become and this year these plants and crops didn't get my part. So they have grown only on outside their roots are week and these roots are not sufficient to take the required minerals from soil and without taking these minerals and essential nutrients from soil how will they have fruit's and grain.

Then the Farmer understands the important lesson in his life. He understands that it was not his care which was giving the fruit's and grains at harvest. It was the strongest winds and rain from god is giving these sweet fruit's and grains.

So the part to learn is that, when these plants and crops face their first wind and rain. It would be hard for them to survive or it would be the toughest time of their life. But once the wind and rain is over these plants understand the adverse situation and work by itself to overcome so that next time when heavy wind or rain hit the farm, they are absolutely ready and those plants and crops which consider this as failure and try to run from it will always face the toughest of the toughest storms and rain fall and these plants and crops will live at the mercy of god or the mercy of these winds or thunderstorms or at the mercy of strong plants which can protect them.

If you run from the situation. One day you can survive or one week or maximum of some months, after that these failures will attack from everywhere and you will not have any place to hide yourself. So to live as a winners or achievers life you have to face the most devastating defects.

The most brutal failures will bring the most powerful hero in you. As its said, "Brightest starts shines more in the darkest night". When you work in the sizzling hot summer then rest of all the season will be a peanut for you. But the daring is to have a strong mind set to work under the sun for a full summer and for entire life you can work on any situation and under any condition.

So face all the failures and always keep in mind that the golden words. " I never fail, I pass or I learn". The beautiful answer given by Sir Thomas Edison when he was asked about all the failed tests in the process of making bulb. He told "I never failed 1,000 times. I learned 1,000 ways by which the bulb can't be made". All the failures give you some great lessons as take away. The more you fail the more lessons you can learn and definitely it will bring out the gladiator in you who can face all the situations strongly and never run away. When someone says, I never failed. It simply means that, he never ever tries anything new in his or her life and his or her life is a bubble which can burst at any moment.

Same with the kids who are over protected by their parents and they were not exposed to the real world or exposed to a real situation and always their parents act as a shield whenever these kids fall in some adheres situation and parents will do anything to protect their kids and these kids are pampered from their childhood days to the end of teen age. When these kids grow up and when they are left alone in the real world they struggle to core as their shield is not there and they are exposed to the world. Same like a computer which was protected by Antivirus software and the entire virus were eagerly waiting outside the door for the Antivirus to turn off or it goes expired. Once that happen, all frustrated, violent, merciless virus which were waiting outside the door will attack with all its force and from everywhere to crash the system completely. It would be hard for the boy to survive as his or her parents taught them how to crack a problem in maths or how to crack CAT MAT or IIT. But they missed to teach how to crack problem a real life situation. There he or she will be an utter failure and all the dreams of parents and kids were shattered at the very next moment when these kids' faces the real world.

Parents can provide a silent environment for their kids to study at exam time. They will cut the Cable connection and all the mobiles where silent and Face book and Wats up and all social media apps where deleted from mobile for one or two months it will be pin drop silent and even the mother washes vessels slowly and carefully so that not even that voice will reach up to the study room and at the exam day, the kid had got an exam centre where nearby construction site and it's too noisy and this kid who had been trained in closed sound proof rooms and in Air Conditioner is suddenly exposed to an open exam hall with a fan which just rotate to prove that it is not dead and while rotating you can easily count the wings and its size and the number of dots in the wings and the heavy noise from the construction sites near by the school campus.

At that time you will see the conspiracy of god kept for us, these labours where so energized and so passionate towards the work that they will bang hammers on steel like Sunny Deols "Dhai Kilo ka hath" and the supervisor was running and shouting and giving instruction to the workers at top of his voice, Feels like the Pakistan Army had reached our boarder and he is the Commander in chief of the pivotal point and gives instructions to his fellow Army men and the entire country's eyes are on him. Instructions are given at top of his voice and after the exam when you are leaving the room, just look at them. The workers are working slowly and without making any noise as if they are hearing Jagjeet Singh's song and the Supervisor our Commander in Chief will be holding a cup of tea in one hand and a cigarette in another sitting quietly at a corner of the construction site, looking at sky as if he had found his first love and he and his crush is dancing on " Pehala Nasha, Pahala Khuma" and the entire scene at the construction site will make you feel like a haunted and abandoned mansion.

So the point is, what do you expect from a kid who studied in a close room for months for this exam and the exam centre is in the middle of a mess. Does he would be concentrate on the exam and does he would be able to write the answers peacefully or at least does he will remember the answer in the mid of this mess.

All the efforts put for the past many months gone in vain in a matter of two three hours. Whom to blame.

So live in real world and from childhood days onwards, face the real situation and face real problem and don't cry for Mummy or Daddy. Even kids cry for parent, don't give them hand to stand up. If you give hand one time, kids always expect and one day they find that the hand is not there to help them. They will panic, as they don't know. how to rise from the situation and at the moment, if any one who gives the hand. Kids will find them as a saviour and follow that person even if the person is taking them to the dark world. They don't Care. They only see the helping hand they got when they require and these kids won't think much.

I am telling it from my experience. As I studied from 11th to my graduation in an hostel where I have seen many cases like this. To all Parents, let our kids fall and you can watch it from a distance. Let them stand and come out of it. Give them advice but don't cover them. So that whenever the fall in life. They will not expect you to come and hold their hands. They will only hear to your advice which you have given in past and that is what is required for them to come up, stand and they fly again.

Composition of all Emotions

There are many types of emotions and our mind and brain is set to have one of these emotions at any point of time.

Generally the emotions are happiness, sadness, disgust, fear, surprise, and anger . It is very much fine, if we have these emotions running and changing itself in our mind. Problem starts when the negative emotions starts to dominate our mind and our self and it over shadow all the other emotions with in us. Life is all about controlling your emotions and it should be us who should control the emotions in life. It shouldn't be the other way, where our emotions are controlling us and we are living on the mercy of these emotions.

Most of us know, when we start our job and slowly the complexity of the job started to increase and we started getting pressure of the job and pressure from clients, Management and Team lead and when we are victim of the silly politics in the team. These things starts trigger our negative emotions like sadness, disgust, fear and anger and as we are spending our most of the hours on a day in the office, more than half of the good time in a day we spend for the company. On a daily basis, if we have these negative emotions in mind. It will engulf all the positive emotions and slowly it will eat all our happiness and we start looking the world with a negative attitude. Our mind will interpret everything in a negative manner. Even if someone is doing a good dead without expecting anything towards us. We will start looking the person with a doubt. Why he is so nice to me, is he expecting any favour from me or is he playing games with me or does he fooling me or there is something which I am not understanding. We will start looking everything negative side. Even you are given a bright sun in hand, you will try to find its darkness. The 99.09% of light we won't see at that time. It's the 0.01 % of darkness that we will try to see and will make a mountain out of the mole.

If we, who is programmed our mind to look only the negative side of everything and project that as it's quality. It's stated by surveys also, that those people who had jobs which they are not happy with will have a bad or unhappy family life too.

When I was in Dubai, I was staying in a flat along with four other friends. We were very much happy with the life there. Everyone goes to work on the morning and evening we all come back almost at the same time and together we make food and spend some time talking and pulling legs of each other and at week end had some good booze parties at the terrace of the flat. Life was going good and we are so relaxed in life.

One of my roommate, who was very much ambitious in life and have very much clear plans about his future. It was him who had taught us how to look and work for the future. He got a job in an MNC. The MNC where he got the job is the place where almost everyone in Dubai dream to be in. Decent salary, perks and other allowance. He was so excited that he was not able to control his emotions and we all were happy for him. We knew that some or the other day, he will get a job in a big firm and he will prove himself.

Life started moving as usual and me and rest of my two roommates, life was as usual but for him, it was not the same. He slowly started to maintain a distance from us. He was not much involved in cooking as most of the time, he started coming late from work even if he comes early he would open his Laptop and sit there and say, that he had his dinner from outside and started omitting the booze party slowly. Not completely, but the occurrence to attend the party become minimal.

First we used to ask him "is everything all right". He would smile and say that everything is fine and slowly we reached to a conclusion that his ego is restricting him from mingling with us. He might have good decent, cultured friends in his office and we might not be up to his expectation. It hurt us a little but we all were happy for him. No regrets from our end too.

Previously it was four member in one room, then it changed to 3 + 1 member in one room. The new situation become normal new and slowly it become normal and continue for two or three months.

One weekend night, we were sitting in our Terrace and enjoying the cool breeze and the bottle of beer. He came to us silently and sat next to us. The lively environment we have become quite and it was a feeling that a stranger is sitting near to us to overhear what we are talking. We also became silent and it continues for some minute and we can feel that he want to say something to us but the starting problem. His fear how we will react. He want to start the conversation, but fear is not allowing him. We can feel his struggle to talk. Then he burst and started crying and at the situation he was not able to speak and he wants to control his tears which he is not able to do.

We all sat near to him and asked what happened and after getting back to normal, he started explaining about the mental torcher he is undergoing in the work place, from his manger and the discrimination shown by his team member towards the new member and the over load of the work which he needs to complete every day and crucifying him for all the silly errors he makes. Then we understand, it was not the ego which is building walls around us and him. It was the extensive pressure the organisation is giving to him and feel sorry for him and after giving him advice as friends, which is what friends are very good at. He become normal and from that day onwards, we used to take special care of our friend and make sure to spend a high quality time of one or two hours daily with him who is having eight to nine hours of pressure in office. He used to tell each and every thing about his office and we used to laugh at his boss and make some jokes at his team members and slowly he is back to normal.

Our friend understands one thing which was learning for us too. If you think you have a bad day in office, it's a wrong thought. You don't have a bad day in office. You had encountered some bad hours on a day and rest it's up to you how you want to make it. You can carry the negative energy or the badness from office and you can make the entire day bad or after swiping out from office you can swipe out all your bitter moments and look forward for the exciting hours that is ahead of you. Just separate the Bad from the Day and add more fun to the rest of the day. Our friend had tried it and we also helped him and situation changed.

If suppose, he never shared his situation with us. we might assume something else and he will suffer the mental trauma or tension for no reason and it will create a big gap between us and him and slowly his nature tend to shift to the negative side and after some time his mind will accept it and he will be completely changed to a negative or pessimistic person and after a point, it would be difficult to get him back as the same person. On the worst case scenario. Once he gone beyond the saturation point, then he might think of committing suicide or for weak hearts, they may lose their mental stability.

When you have immense pressure at office and you are like a pressure cooker who had taken enough pressure and can burst at any time and with that pressure cooker you are coming to home and you see your kids are making noise or your kid came to you happily and hug you or your wife asking, have you bought the Grocery items which she had given the list in the morning. That's it, all your frustration, anger everything will erupt out of your mind and you will find yourself shouting at your wife or beating your kid and in turn making the peaceful and positive environment of the home to a war zone and after that a dead silence. Your kid will be crying at one corner and your wife will be sitting sadly on another corner and you will be beating your head on the wall on another corner.

If you have opened the pressure cooker the moment you finish your work by sitting quietly and talking to yourself and pepping up your mood, motivating yourself and burry all the bad moments from your mind and from your thoughts and the only thought should be the smile of your kid or your wife or your friends who is waiting for you at home and wash your face. Take a deep breath for three four time. Omit all negative energy and enjoy each and every moment, when travelling back to home. Just look at the people around you, watch their expression and moods and see the beautiful trees, birds and blue sky with white clouds. By the time you reach home, you will be an entire different person and then you will enjoy double or triple for rest of the day and your bad hours are compensated more than expected with your good hours and next day, it's a new beginning.

The day is never bad or the hours are never bad. It's all about how we interpret it. If you consider darkness as end of life, then it's an end of life for you. But if you consider darkness as the beginning of a new day. Then you will never be dishearten or discouraged with the darkness in life. It's our interpretation of different situation which makes a difference in our life.

It's like, Some people believes Cold exist in this world but some people believes the absence of heat is cold and cold doesn't exist in this world. some people believe darkness exist in this world and some people believe there is no darkness in the world, absence of light is darkness and darkness doesn't exist in this world. This world is made up by unlimited colour by god and never added darkness to this world. It's we who had added darkness by switching off all the lights around us. Light from family, light from friends, light from nature, light from all the tiny tiny moments of our life. We switched off all the lights and make it dark and again we complain that my life is full of darkness. Discover the tiny moments of life and live those moments to the fullest and never allow the darkness to conquer your life.

It's we who decide, weather my life should be full of darkness or I will never allow to turn off the lights in my life and never allow the darkness to conquer me or I will never make the darkness so powerful entity who can drag me to its world.

One more thing, we can't avoid all the emotions. We can't avoid negative emotions as its part and parcel of the game. When you hold your negative emotions to yourself and start thinking about it again and again, it starts to conquer your mind and slowly it start controlling you. I believe, we have to face all the emotions and can't run from it. Face the emotions and make sure to control the emotions and don't let the emotions control you.

It's said that, don't make any promises when you are too much happy and don't curse any one when you are too angry. On both case you will regret later. So control your emotions, if you feel angry or frustrated from a situation then immediately take a break or get away from the situation for five or ten minutes and when you think you are back to normal then face the situation. On the five to ten minute, just be with yourself in an empty space and cherish all the wonderful moments you had in your life and rewind all the good memories and I am sure your anger will fly away for ever.

How lethal or dangerous the bowler in cricket, he only get six ball to throw at you and a maximum of sixty ball in a day. If you get disappointed with the six ball and got out. You are missing the part time bowlers whom you can hit six sixes in an over. So defence the six balls from the lethal bowler and enjoy the rest of the innings. Sound so easy, believe me. It's not that hard too. It's all about how willing are we trying it. We have given our control to the emotions and emotions are controlling us.

Just suppose, when you wear a new dress which you were planning to buy for a long time and it's the design which you are trying for the first time and you feel so good and confident wearing the dress and the moment when you walk towards the office, one of your friend says negative about the dress or a bunch of your colleagues looks at you and pass some comments between them and you think they are making fun of your new dress. These small things make you upset and your mood will be gone to ever time low and you blame yourself for buying this dress. Within one minute you forget the happiness you had, when you see yourself in this dress in front of the mirror. Just because some tom dick and harry made some comments, why I should feel low. It's my choice and it's my life dude.

When someone says something pin pointing against you or on a group you have been targeted and your friends are pulling your legs and these small things make you upset. Not even your friends, anyone in the world can make you upset and have the capability to feel you low. Not getting enough likes and comments on the photo you uploaded in Facebook or Instagram etc can upset your mood.

Just think, is my emotions so cheap that anyone can play with it. Anyone can destroy my mood or my emotions just like that. If the answer is yes, then it's time to think about this seriously. First thing we have to understand we are living in a society where peoples are civilized but the DNA of every one is same. Where everyone is trying to survive or to win the race on the cost of others loss or by stepping on others back or head. If you have to win then every one has to lose. A complex game with simple rule. From our childhood days we are thought to came first on the exam and win all the competitions you participate. If you want to be recognised as a good student then you have to make sure that everyone is in the class is bad. The rule is set not by us. It's set from the ancient times and we are following the same. It's not possible to come first, if everyone is equal competent and have the same knowledge of all the rules and regulations of the game. So you have to play psychologically to throw them away from the game and if your competitor realise that you are an highly emotional and can be easily carried away with small small issue. So why in the entire world, I shouldn't use it as a weapon against you. I will play mind games to make you mentally and emotionally week and slowly I will create the entire possible adverse situation against you to make you feel low and so dejected which will compel you to think to quite the competition. It's the wild jungle rule that applies here. Survivor of the fittest and if you don't know how to survive in between these beasts then they will brutally kill you from inside. Understand the bitter truth; there are no well-wishers for you in this world. Everyone who is associated with you are associated for a reason. If the reason is not satisfied they will move away from you without saying a good bye. Your friends are associated with you because they are expecting a moral or mental support from you. The moment you stop giving the support they will not stick with you. How many of you are in touch with your collage or school friends. I mean with the same intensity of friendship. When we get new friends, we tend to forget our old friends and even our first crush.

So my point is, in a selfish world you are expecting affection or whole hearted appreciation will be like sitting under the mango tree and waiting for an earthquake, so that all mangoes will fall down and you can gather mangoes from ground. If you accept this fact of life, then never ever you will be dishearten or demotivated on a negative comment from your colleague on the new dress or harsh comments from your manager or when your friends making fun of you in a group or bullying you in school or college. Anything happens you know who you are and what is your calibre and potential. I wear the new dress because I love it and I don't care what other think, if my friends are making fun of me in front of everyone, it's because they are jealous of me, if I am being ragged or bullied in school or college, try to enjoy it or take it in positive sense and learn the technique of ragging or bullying, so that next year you can use the same.

Always tell your mind that, there is no one in the entire world who can make me sad or demotivated. I control my life and dam care about others comment. No one can control me. When I feel to be sad, I will be sad. But I will never be sad or cry on some other person's comments or dialogues. I didn't give the privilege to anyone in the entire world to make me sad or demotivated. This privilege is with me and will always be with me only till I die. Train your mind and see the difference.

Don't forget one thing, don't supress any emotions inside you. Release all the emotions otherwise, as I told you about the pressure cooker. The pressure of supressed emotions will reach to a saturation point and will burst and it can harm you, your family and your friends etc.

Everyone have a composition of emotions. It's like the percentage of happiness, sadness, anger, anxiety etc. All the emotions have a percentage within you. There will not be zero for any emotions. It's us who makes the composition. Person who selects Anger -> 60% rest distribute among other emotions will always be unhappy with his life and will have high BP and he can be a potential candidate for a heart attack and will have all the health disorder which a person can have. So keep in mind to keep the positive emotions at high stake so that every day, every minute you enjoy your life to the core.

Power of belief

It's said that, what we believe is what we are. It's a very true statement. It's the mind which forms our nature and our beliefs and the input that we give to our mind will be slowly converted to our nature and habit. So we should pay good attention to the input that we give to our mind.

Have you ever noticed that, at our childhood days when we were in school and we got average marks. Not good to be a topper or not bad to be a dropper and our teacher regularly told us directly or indirectly that you are an average student to us and to our parents and our parents also conveyed the same message to us that you are an average student and slowly our mind started accepting the input that you are an average student and from that time till now you are just an average student. Hope many of you have noticed this trend in their academic life. Once in a blue moon we might top on one or the other subject but generally for all the subjects we were not at the bottom or not at the top. It's the same for the toppers and the class lowest scorers.

Have you ever tried to understand one thing. On all the exams for all the different subjects the questions will be different and evaluating teachers will be different and on all the classes the curriculum will change but to our wonder our scores would be almost the same. It won't change much. Every thing change, class, teachers, teaching style, syllabus, friends, way of learning everything will change but one thing which will not change is the trend of score that we get on each exams. It would be somewhat same.

It's because when your mind accept the fact that you are an average student. Mind will take bare effort to get an average score. It won't take much effort to bring you A+ Scores. Here the instruction is set from childhood days onwards and this average student attitude will continue in our professional life and we accept and agree with the fact that I am an ordinary student or an ordinary employee and I can't go beyond a particular point which is been set as a finishing line for me.

Exceptions are there, when you are insulted in class or by your parents for scoring low marks which spark the emotions in you and you put your heart and soul to reach to the topper and if you reach there then it's a new input which is been given to the mind and it will start to re program all the set programs and there would be a drastic change in those students. But that situation happens once in a blue moon, as we have already compromised with what we have.

It's the human nature of laziness to accept what nature and the world throws at us without giving a minimum fight or resistance and very proudly say, I am happy with what I have. This is my limit and I can't go beyond it. I deserve better than this but my life is cruel to me so I am good with it. Believe me, these are the words of losers who know that it's their fault but again don't want to take blame on themselves. They know they are the culprit, but they blame everyone in the world. Everything was wrong with them but they are right. That type of mind set can't be changed and day by day the walls around the mind-set becomes so strong that putting a new input to the mind takes a lot of effort. The voice will not reach to the mind though these iron walls. After a time, it would be an impossible task to change the current mind set.

These people live life for the sake of living and they are the wooden loft which floats on water and it can flow to any direction depending up on the current of the water and these wooden loft doesn't have any aim and it's happy to go with water and where ever the water drop these wooden loft, they will consider it as their destination and lives a peaceful life there without any complain or trying to improve the standard. They can't fight against anything in life. It's our belief which makes us week and it's the same belief which can bring out the Super man or Wonder women in you. If we understand that all the human beings are filled with unlimited possibilities we won't believe as we haven't seen the possibilities and we have taught from the earlier stages to only believe what is seen by your naked eyes never believe anything else.

Before the invention of bicycle, if someone have told you that there is a gadget which we can use to go to places. Everyone would laugh on it. Before the inventions of Aeroplane, if someone have told that there is a flying machine which can fly on its own without flapping wings and we can also travel on it. We would think that the person who is telling these is an insane. This is because we don't want to see outside the box which we are fit in currently and that the box we are fit in is a dark room and without any ray of light or hope. The more you live in that room the more you will fell to the trap and that dark room will make your mind blind from inside. You can see the world but your mind can't see or explore the new world. That dark room has killed all the sense organs of our mind and its wings too. So the rest of your life, you will live a life in that dark room without any hope without any dream or without any aspiration in life. It's not because we don't have to capability to all these, it's because we have forgot to come out.

So come out of the room and see the beautiful world out there. Explore the unexplored, question the un question, debate on un debated topics, see the unseen world, feel the un felled emotions experience the un conditional love and affection and give away the unnecessary ego from life and learn new and exciting things and on one word. Be yourself. The more you explore yourself the more you will find the difference between the You till yesterday and the you on today and don't ever draw a pre calculated picture of yours. Your current status is not the final picture of yours. Nature need to add more colours to it only if you allow.

There is story in the Hindu mythology, Ramayan. Hanuman was gifted with super powers which no one else in the earth had in his time but he had got a curse in his childhood days that he will forget his powers and he will remember only when someone reminds his power. So in search of Sita, Ram Lakshma and the entire ape force came till Ramaswaram and from that place they have to cross an Ocean to go to Srilanka and before the entire force proceed towards Sri Lanka someone has to confirm if the Sita is there in Srilanka or not. Everyone was sitting and thinking, who will cross the Ocean and how to get to know the presence of Sita in Srilanka. Along with everyone Hanuman was also sitting and thinking. By that time, Jambavanta the king of bear came to Hanuman and he started telling the powers Hanuman possess. At first Hanuman was not taking it seriously and later Hanuman started believing the words of Jambavanta and he started identifying the unlimited potential powers which he hold with in him and till now he was not aware of it. The moment Hanuman had the self-realisation he started believing in his power and crossed the Ocean by flying with the help of his powers and reach Srilanka and meet Sita. If Jambavanta was not there and he didn't mind to explain the power he possess then for the whole life Hanuman will be thinking that he is just an ordinary ape and will die as an ordinary ape. But the moment he started believing in himself and his powers, he was able to cross the ocean without any ones help and destroyed half of the Srilanka, meet Sita in between the tight security and came back without a single scratch on his body.

The problem with us is that, we don't have a Jambavanta who can tell or make us realise our high potential energy or the super power we have. We all are waiting for the Jambavanta in our life to tell us about the super power we hold and only a very people in the world will get that opportunity where some or the other form Jambavanta will come and tell about their power.

But in every once life, there is an opportunity when we confront with our potential energy or power in some or the other way. Some identifies and take it as an opportunity and work on it and many don't mind it or understand and move forward with the same state of mind.

If the Ticket checker in the Indian Railway didn't believed the potential and the super power he had towards the cricket then we might never had seen MS Dhoni playing for India. We might only have seen the Ticket Checker who don't realise the potential in him and compromised his life towards a government job. He had two options like I mentioned above. Take it as an opportunity and work on it or move with the life, as if nothing has happened.

Belief has a tremendous power in itself. It is not as simple or small as it looks like. In India at festival season, you might have seen people piercing iron or steel sticks in tongue or steel hooks are pierced in the body and with a chain attached to the hook they will be lifted to air. The person who sees it feel the pain but if you see the person whose body is pierced will be calm and quite. Have you ever dare to pierce a steel stick into your tongue or to both the cheeks.

It's their belief, they believe that they are pleasing god by taking all the pain and their belief is so deeply rooted in their mind that they don't feel the pain. They only see it as blessing of god and they are meant to perform this act to make the god happy. On doing the task they only see the power of blessing that they will get not the tremendous pain which they have to go through. Every year you can the same people doing the same act. That's the belief. Same theory is used by Terrorists group also. These groups make the terrorists who crosses boarder for a reason that they are doing it for a purpose and the purpose is the ultimate thing and all the pains or grievances are very minute when compared to their purpose.

So as I mentioned the belief has an unlimited potential to break or to make you. Most of us know, in office or outside when we meet some guy or lady who speaks fluent English and well groomed and have a fair completion and talk with high confidence. When we talk to them we feel we are smaller to them and the long the conversation goes, we feel we are shrinking more and more in front of them.

We think it's their look or it's their influence over us makes us feel low or small or it's their charisma which feel our self-small in front of them . But the truth is that we are getting smaller or feel low in front of them. We are the same but we are making them big. We consider that their attributes or traits are much higher than us and their standard is very high than us and we make them much higher when compared to our self.

Have you seen the Bahubali 2 movie. On that there was a scene where the big statue of Bhalal Dev is being placed and all the labours are towing the rope attached to the status and suddenly one person sees Bahubali and he started shouting " Bahubali, Bahubali" and every one started chanting Bahubali and Bhalal dev happens to hear the slogan everyone is shouting and screaming and he can see visualize the version of the status with Bahubali's image and the image was getting bigger and bigger and it became so big that it touches the sky and in front of Bahubali's status his status was just a small toy.

That's the same feeling we have which brings the inferiority complex in us or the feel of un secureness in our mind which make us feel the status of others look big when compared to ours. As I mentioned earlier, it's just because we haven't explored the powers and potentials we hold and we are only looking outside and seeing the powers of others.

It's like living on a gold mine and spending the hard earn money to buy one gram of gold not realising that under you is the most expensive gold mine.

There was a beautiful story I happened to hear. A person who was dejected in life came to a Guru and asked the Guru, what is my value in this world. Is my value in this world is nil, please explain me Guru.

Guru smiled and given him a shining diamond and told. You take this diamond and go the market and ask all the vendors the value of the diamond but don't sell this to anyone.

As said by Guru he goes to the market and he found a fruit seller and shown him the diamond and ask how much you will pay me for this diamond. The fruit seller told that I can give you one kilo gram orange and one kilo gram apple if you give this diamond to me.

He thanked the fruit vendor for the deal and started walking and he came to a textile vendor and asked the same question. The textile vendor told that I can give two Saree for this diamond and again he thanked him for the deal and started walking and the third was a vegetable vendor and asked the same question and he was ready to give five kilo grams of all vegetables he had. Shown it to Ironsmith and he told he don't require it but as it's a shining metal which I don't have any use but I can buy it for my wife and give you two big knife against it.

On last he went to a diamond merchant and ask what's the offer he can me. The diamond merchant after scanning the diamond with his magnifying glass and seeing all the sides of diamond straight offered him one million and the person was shocked and surprised. He thanked Diamond merchant and started walking, diamond merchant stopped and told him. Give me this diamond and I can give you half of my property and the person again started walking and diamond merchant makes a deal and told I can give my entire property which is worth of millions and I can give all my diamond collection and I can give you this shop and if you want more I can give my brothers property which also cost millions to you but please give me that diamond. The man told that he don't own the diamond it's the diamond of his Guru and he had given this to me for a reason and he went back to his guru and told everything in detail what has happened in the market and Guru told him the important lesson of his life.

We don't come with a price tag or a value it's where we want to sell our self. The fruit vendor doesn't understand the value of the diamond so he made a simple offer and if you have sold the diamond for some fruit's you would never understand the true value of diamond and for you the value of diamond will be one kilo gram of apple and one kilo gram of orange and same if you have sold to a textile vendor then you think the value of diamond is worth of a saree and if you have sold the diamond to a vegetable vendor then you think the value of the diamond is worth some vegetables.

But when you went to the diamond merchant you realise the actual value of the diamond. It's price less. The diamond merchant knows the value of diamond and he know that he don't have the asset or money to pay for the diamond so he offered his brothers too and he still know that it can't compensate the value of the diamond.

You are diamond in the story and just think to whom you are selling yourself. To those people who doesn't understand your value and potential and always make you feel low and small or to those who admire your value and respect you sincerely. For that as a diamond you have to find your value and should identify where you have to sell yourself.

Don't be a diamond with the fruit vendor or with the textile vendor or with the vegetable vendor. Always be a diamond with the diamond merchant and increase your value day by day that even the diamond merchant will not be able to buy you.

So the summarize the topic, it's what we believe what we are. So believe high and more importantly believe in yourself. You are the unique creation of god. If god had created you in the way you are now which means he has a purpose attached to it.

Have we ever realised that, we say we are an individual human being or an individual entity in this world, but have you noticed that there are a million similarities you have with your parents, grant parents, great and great great grandparents. Which is not coincidences. We might think that our life is isolated and we are not answerable to anyone. Which is not true. In Hindu mythology its believe that we carry the genes of our seven generations in our body. That's why there our good or bad karma will affect us in positive or negative manner. Which means your action will impact your next seven generations to come. These may be a point of debate which we can debate later. As I know many of you won't believe in these. There is no proof to substantiate any of these and it's called as a superstition. But if I look like my Grand father then there is some connection between me and him.

If an apple didn't have fallen into Newton's head then Gravity also might be a superstition. But the fact is that before the apple fall and after the apple fall there was Gravity and till the date it was recognised by a person, it was a superstition and after its recognised and given a name it become part of science.

Now we have only two division or two side of the coin. If anything that can be explained by science is good to believe and anything which can't be explained by science is super natural or superstition.

On Full Moon day, oceans and sea experience Neap Tides. Which Science explains as gravitational pull of Moon. Which will be again a superstation, if Gravity was not been discovered by Issac Newton. If a Full Moon can impact the water which is more than 70% of our earth, so just imagine, how much effect it can be on our body which is having around 70% of water. It may effect Heart, Brain, Kidney and Blood pressure. It may highly influence your mood, behaviour, anxiety, stress etc.

So my point is, an entity which is so far from earth can impact so much on a single night then just imagine what all factor in our earth or the nature around us can impact us.

The seed in my pocket

As we all know there are two types of people in the world, Dreamers and Doers. If we divide these two type of people. Dreamers' population would be the highest. It will occupy around 99% of the population. Every second person in this world will fall under this category and more over Dreamers looks alike, not with their facial features but with the habit and attitude they have. You can easily identify these dreamers just with a single glance of look. They all do the same think talk same language. They are like a clone of one another. These are the people who start their life at one point and after many years they realise they have forgot put the 1st gear and they are simply raising the accelerator for no reason and getting happy to hear the sound of the motor roaring. For a long time they even don't understand that their vehicle had not even moved an inch and by the time they understand, they had the habit of driving a stand still vehicle and the heights of laziness has reached to the level that they started making excuses for not changing the gear.

Dreamers are like the swimmer who stands at the sea shore and waiting for the last tide to hit the shore then to have a peaceful swim. They dream of swimming in the tide less sea and they can wait for any number of days, hoping there will be a day when the sea will be quite and they can have a dream swim.

But doers on other hand, they love swimming on the tides. They are always ready to confront with the biggest tide at any time. They always have plan for their swimming. They strictly stick with their plans and always try to put heart and soul to any activity they do. They live along with us. But they are actually not concerned about the current life or its current situation. As they had killed there current me for a better me.

Our dreams are like a seed of a tree. It can be seed of any tree. The point is that how are you handling the seed. We the majority of the population which we described as Dreamers would like to put the seed in pocket and walk the entire life thinking that my dreams have not come true. Everyone else had succeeded in their life and I am left alone. We cry, get annoyed and get frustrated after a long time and leave the track and settle for whatever we get. Even if I didn't get anything I will quite the game of running behind the dream. But we never think that the seed of the dream which I am searching in the entire world is still lying in my pocket and it's untouched.

When you identify your seed of the dream then instead of keeping in the pocket. Find a fertile soil to put the seed and water it for some days. Some seeds may show up quickly in form of plant others will take its own sweet time. But water them regularly and once it show up the soil then build a protective cover or a boundary so that no one can touch, spoil or break the plant and give fertilizer and take care of the small plant like how a mother take care of its baby. Give water, sunlight and food when it's necessary and always take care of its surrounding. Protect it from bugs and from adverse climate. In short be like a passionate gardener who is ready to give everything for the plant. Then only after some time, you can start getting the fruits of your effort and you will get the fruit for your life time.

Same like, when you have a dream and you are sure it's the dream which you bet anything to it including your life. Why I am stressing is that, the dream which you are going to put your heart and soul should be quantifiable.

We can dream too many things. I want to be a millionaire. After watching a cricket match, I want to be Virat Kohli or Dhoni or after watching any movie I want to be like the hero of the movie and many more. These are dreams which can't be quantifiable. If you have some solid plans to be a millionaire or have a passion to be cricketer or footballer then it's great. It's your seed of dream. Go for it.

So identify the seed of your dream. Then find some fertile soil which will be your dedicated time and your plans to work for the dream. As I mentioned earlier, what all plan you are making, make sure it doesn't have much options. Once I start to work on my dream. It should be Do or Die. No other options should be valid. On 24 hour clock you should have to find descend time for your dream or goal on daily basis. It should be like, if I can find time for myself to have food three to four times a day then why can't I find time for my dreams. If I didn't get the time to work on my dream. I will eat only two times and get the time from there. If anyone reading this thinks it as craziness then I would like to say that without madness and craziness you can't get the key of your dream.

There is only a small bunch of people whom world first believed as mad and made fun of them. Then later entire world stood in front of them and saluted them. Those are the people who identify the seeds of dream and worked like crazy. They felt in deep love with their dream and the love was so deep that they can live without food or shelter but they can't live without their dream.

Once you give proper and dedicated time to your dream then it's your duty of you to take care of your dream. Give motivation and inspiration and get boast yourself frequently. In short, live in your dream.

I had a session with class 10th students, where I asked them what you want to become in future. As 10th is considered as turning point of your career. As expected everyone told Doctor, Engineer, Pilot, Astronaut etc. Then I asked, how many of you believe that you are a Doctor, Engineer or pilot now. As expected it's a pin drop silence to the question. I know it's a wired a question to ask. But as I said earlier. It's all about living in the dream. If I don't believe that I am a Doctor today. How will I be having the passion to be a doctor tomorrow. Before you start arguing with me in this point. I want to tell you a story.

It's from Mahabharata, there was a boy called Ekalavya. Who was the young prince of a small tribe and he was from a low caste, who want to learn Archery. He was rejected by Drona who was the greatest coach of all time. He was so passionate of the Archery and he lives and sees himself as a great archer. After rejected by Drona he didn't quite his dream by giving any excuse. He made a clay model of Drona and accept Drona as his coach. In front of the clay model he started learning Archery by himself and his skills where unmatched to any of the great archers living at that era and when Drona came to know about his skills he also got astonished and more than the fear that Arjuna losing in front of Ekalavya made him to ask his thumb finger as fees which without a second though Ekalavya gives to Drona. As in Archary thumb finger plays a vital role and without thumb finger an Archer is nothing.

This seems just like an another story. But the story of Ekalavya has so much to tell. It's a story of a boy who had a dream and identified a school where he can go and achieve his goal. But got rejected for a reason which he is not responsible for. It's a dead end for his dream. If he wants, he could have quite his dream and blamed Drona or God. Of course, if he does it then he can't be blamed also. But he decided not to quite the dream and started practicing with all potential and all energy he had. Daily practiced, practiced, practiced, practiced and reached to the level that the greatest master of Archery Arjuna and the man behind making the greatest archer got their shock of life.

Ekalavya has all the right in the world to keep his seed of dream in pocket and live a normal life but he chose to fight all the odds which comes against him and his passion towards the Archary and his love and respect towards the Drona was so deep and can't be narrated in any scripture. He didn't think twice before cutting the thumb finger which he knows, it's the end of his passion and dream. That's the height of passion.

The heights of passion can't be measured by any scale. It's always broken by some or other crazy or mad person who dare to go to the extreme and again the height it's broken by another. So the height of passion will always be broken till the last day of human existence in this world. Only question which remain is that. Do you dare to break the height or not. Do you have to passion to do it or not. If the answer is yes, then we can continue.

If you are feeling sleepy, you can go and wash your face with cold water, as I am going to do the same and planning to have a cup of tea. Which I am not at all passionate in making.

Oh boy, not a bad tea. Now I realise, necessity makes us do new things and slowly we master it.

Another point is that, once you identify your dream, you have to protect it from bugs, animals, insects and the adverse natural conditions which means, there will many people or situations which will try to pull you down. We discussed this earlier also. But with context to the topic, I am writing again.

Just now I have a made a nice cup of tea for myself which gained my confidence in preparing the tea and slowly I gained the confidence day after day by preparing tea for myself but if some guests comes to my house and with the confidence I gained over past few days, I prepared them tea and two three members gives negative comments at time. Then I am done. I will never try to make tea for others. All my confidence will be vanished without leaving a trace.

You will find many peoples or situation or the nature which may try to pull you down. So prepare for these situation in advance and always say to yourself. That my dream is my property where I am working hard to make a mansion and I don't rent my property to others to make their Public Comfort room.

Till the time you think, at most care is required for your dream give it on the same passion the mother gives love and affection to its kids. Once the root of dreams gets deeply rooted in the soil which is your mind and brain, till then give good care.

Then what your mind will work to complete the dream. Now it's part of your habit and now you can relax and enjoy the fruits of your dream for entire life.

Equation is simple. Work hard now and relax for rest of your life or relax now and work hard for rest of your life. Answer is with you. No one will care, if you chose the second one but people forcefully need to care about you, if you choosing the first option.

So to brief the point. All of us have the seed of dreams with us. It's us who decide to keep it in pocket or to find some soil and put it and allow it grow into trees. What all you decide? Just understand one thing; your single decision can change the pace of your life. It can make or break you. So decide wisely and more important think twice before you act.

Acquire skills from others

As we are part of the society which plays an important role in moulding us. Our nature our habits our ego our attitude etc are so much influenced by our friends and family.

From childhood days we had a habit of imitating others. If you see small kids you can easily relate what I am talking about. They are very good at imitating. Through imitating we learned everything including the language we speak. When we get older most of our habits changes but our habit of imitating remains with us which can do good or bad, depending upon the company of people we are daily interacting with. Even a movie has the power to influence us.

Suppose, if we can use this inbuilt ability which we carry from our childhood days as a powerful weapon to develop our self, then it would be an easy win and anyone can do it without any cost.

Before I proceed further, I want to tell a story.

In Hindu mythology, Goddess Durga is considered as the most powerful goddess. She had been given the task to kill the demon king called Mahisasura. Who was the most powerful demon on earth. As he got a boon that he can't be killed by a man. He defeated everyone who came in his way and the tension was building everywhere in earth and in heaven.

So to kill the demon Load Indra give Goddess Durga Vajra ayudh (thunder bolt wepon), Varuna give her his conch, Vayu dev (god of wind) gives her bow and arrows and Vishwakarma give her his Axe and armour and Load of the mountain give her a Lion and Load Shiva give her his Trishul Vishnu give his Sudarna chakra, Brahma give kamandal and these weapons increased her power to infinity and the battle was fought between the Goddess and Mahishasur for around ten days and she killed the demon. Even now Goddess Durga is considered as symbol of power.

Now coming to the crux of the story. We all have a negative side and a positive side. In short we all have Durga and Mahishasur within us. It's a battle which is happening within us between our negative and the positive me. A battle which started from our childhood days and stills it's going on. Still there is a ray of hope that good or positive can beat the evil or negative me. Only thing which we have to do is that we have to find the weapons from our surroundings which can beat the evil in me.

How can I find it? It's quite simple. I am surrounded by peoples who have these weapons and my duty is to just acquire it from them. For example, I am working in an office in a team of ten member. Everyone holds different skills and each skills of these ten persons are unique and it's the lethal weapon. No one will give their weapon to you for free as there is no free lunch in this world. You have to observe each of your colleague and identify what are they strong at. Talk to them and identify their unique skills and slowly learn it. Open your mind and get influenced by them.

Disclaimer :- Only accept good skills or nature and omit the bad one.

It's not a one or two day process. It's a continues process throughout the life, which you can use it in your personal and professional life. Talk to people, understand them, relate yourself to them, let them open their heart. Be a good listener and get the maximum from every one. Everyone will have something to give you. Just imagine, if you can open your heart and mind to everyone and listen to their experiences, stories or any skills which they would love to share with you. Go for it.

Without you realising you are developing a super hero inside you who acquire many super powers over these years and fighting its battle of life time and these power will enlighten your life for ever.

Acquire all the small or big weapons from where ever possible and make your armoury the most strongest one. Let these weapon spread the light and power within you. These light and power will be enough for you climb the steps of success, sorry the mountain of success.

Its little bit hard, but the greatest view can be seen after hardest climb. So fasten your seat belt and meet people, that also with an open mind and heart. Then you will experience a different you after some time. You will be the personality who acquired the strongest weapon from the strongest members and fighting against the darkness inside you. A battle which can't be win easily because these darkness has been deeply rooted inside you and need time and have to undergo too much pain to throw it away.

Self Confidence, Self Belief and Self Respect

These three are like inter connected traits, where one leads to other, if all three are achieved then it will transform your life.

Before I start this topic, just want to tell you that what all I am writing is just my understanding which I have observed and I think which are relevant to improve the quality of life , it's my perception which is open to any debate or criticism . As everyone has their own say and understanding which may be different from others.

Twinkle Twinkle little star in a child perception is a like a diamond in the sky, same twinkle star in a romantic couples perception is sign of romance, in the eyes of a emotional person, it's their near and dears who passed away, for Astronomers these Twinkle Twinkle little stars are their bread and butter for Astrologists, used to calculate a persons present and future and for a busy peoples like us who has lots of tension on head it's not more than just an small LED light in sky. We give more importance to the Christmas star which we hang on the Christmas tree or in front of the house when compared to the stars in sky.

So what I am saying is that on each topic we all have our point of view which is not necessary that it should connect with each other. But here I am the author and you are the reader. So I am on a better spot. As you have left with two options. Skip the page on the book or read whatever is there in the book. Just kidding. But if life allows us to meet then we can put both our points and we can have a detailed discussion.

So I was saying that Confidence, belief and respect are three stages or compartments which are inter connected to each other.

When you build confidence in yourself by doing simplest of the simplest task with at most care and by putting your heart and soul to it. Like how simple the task may be, if it's done with full consciousness and with full dedication. Not to satisfy any one else but to prove yourselves that you are highly competent to do any task.

From cleaning the bed in the morning or washing your plate yourself after food to making the biggest presentation to the management or sending monthly or yearly dashboards to the client. If you feel all tasks are of same importance and it need the same conscious effort and you are emotionally connected to all these tasks. Even if it's a few minutes tasks, involve all your senses and give importance to all the tasks. Then before going to bed when you look back the entire day, you will feel the difference. You will feel the extra pinch of joy and completeness that you have put on the day. We always do most of the task for sake of doing and that also without putting consciousness into it.

If I ask you to explain the feeling you had when you were brushing your teeth today morning with the most expensive brush you have bought to have good experience to you and to the teeth and your favourite brand of tooth paste.

Most of us will think, what a creepy question is this. From childhood days we are doing brushing and now it's just a task. Nothing more than that. But just for one day, brush consciously with all senses open and enjoy the brushing sound, enjoy the flavour of the toothpaste and brush slowly and enjoy each and every moment. It would be a different moment all together.

Just putting on simple words. Now we are doing most of our tasks with half-conscious as we are trained on it. I am driving my bike for years. Now I don't have to drive it consciously. Without me realising I will change the gear, I will raise or drop accelerator. It's a semi-conscious act which I am performing daily.

So my point is that, these small small tasks and these small small moments start doing it consciously. Then you will feel like, is it the same task which we were doing for years.

Have you seen English men in movies drinking scotch and whisky. Small sips and enjoy it. Actually like me, many of us started drinking Whisky and Rum by getting inspired by the way they drink. Enjoying each and every sip is a next level feeling. Not like how it's shown in many of the Bollywood movies. Get the bottle and one gulp, drink it completely. I still don't understand who can do it. I tried to drink one peg in a gulp without water and I ran here and there without any reason and I thought my internal organs would be like a burned rubber tyre. I also had next level feeling. I feel that I am finished and not any doctor but only fire force can save me. It was that much burning from inside.

We always eat our food in a hurry or by watching TV or by talking to our family members in the table. While doing that, half of the meal we are eating without realising its actual taste. Instead of that just off your TV and without talking to your family just concentrate on the food. Chew it consciously and as slow as possible. You can feel the taste of each ingredients which is their in the food. These ingredients and the entire food will charge all your taste buds and you will feel like in cloud nine.

So in short, if you do ten tasks in a day. Perform these ten tasks with same enthusiasm and passion. If all these tasks are done with the zeal and perfection, your level of confidence will be sky high.

This will boost your confidence to extreme level. If practice this daily, it will slowly moves to the sub conscious mind and our mind will accept this as our habit and which will boost our self-belief.

I had already mentioned on the self-belief before. But to the context of this topic, thought of adding some more points to it. As I mentioned earlier, what you believe is what you are. As we are living in a wild and brutal jungle. Much dangerous than an actual wild jungle. On the real Jungle, we know who our friends are and who are our enemies. We know how each animal or insects behave and they will behave as expected. We know to which animal we can go nearby and feed and to which animal we have to keep a distance and by seeing which animal we need to run for life.

But in our jungle which is called as civilized society. We still don't who are our enemies and friends. Those who we think are our best friends will turn to be our worst enemies in minutes. We don't know who are planning to attack us. We don't know who are waiting to see our fall. Who all are showing empathy in front of us and stab us on back in very next moment.

Real jungle has a rule and all its inmates follow it too. Even though the rule is not written anywhere. We have a full established wing who had written rules and regulations and we all agree to it and a wing to protect the rule and a wing to prosecute those who break the rule. We know all the rules and its punishment. By having these established systems in place, we still love to break rules for our personal gains. We a civilized member of a civilized society who gives predominate importance to rule of the land and we break it when we feel like to break it.

That's the difference between the wild wild and the civilized wild jungle. In jungle, all the animals know there limitations and their rights. From childhood days they follow the same. Beasts of the jungle hunts it's pray only when they are hungry.

We human are so self-centred animals who always think of themselves first. Who put their own priorities first than others.

Living in a world, between these self-centred people and to build a self-confidence and self-belief and self-respect is not that easy assignment. Where on each and every step you would be pulled down by others. No one will allow you to go to the next step. You have to fight hard to place yourself and keep yourself in the race.

Those who are working in corporate world or in any industry can understand this. Where your mistakes or errors are celebrated by your colleagues and your department. Reason is simple. For example, in a department of ten employees, there will be one supervisor and these ten employees know that to get the promotion or to reach the level of supervisor you need to back stab the other nine employees. You need to prove at any cost that you are the inevitable asset of the department. For that you will play any dirty politics and tricks. No one to blame for, it's the human phycology. That's what we are thought from our child hood days. To win the race or to come first you have to beat everyone. My success lies in the failure of others. We all dream of a high quality of life and to achieve it we need to be selfish and self-centred.

Everyone who is connected to us, our friends, family and relatives and everyone who makes and completes our world are connected to us for a reason. Till the time they are getting what they want, they will be connected to us. Once you stop giving them what they want they will leave us and go.

Like our friends are connected us because they are getting care and support from us. We are their charging stations, they will connect with us when their charge is drained out or they need help and vice versa. The moment we stop speaking to our friends and doesn't give what they need from us they will slowly start moving away from us.

Our wife or girlfriends require loves, care and some dedicated time. If we fail to give, there will be a gap in the relation. Same with all relations. If you stop pumping the fuel of love, care, compassion, emotions, dedication, empathy, sympathy, kindness, consideration, affection, sentiments, passion, understanding, attention, respect, fondness, love, romance then these relationships will come to a dead end. Without these, how strong is the relation be. It will break every effortlessly.

In earlier times of human civilization there exists something called Barter system. It's an exchange of goods and services exchanged for other goods and services. It's like a contract between two parties.

From that time till today. Everything has changed. Telephone has become cell phone. Black and white TV has become smart TV etc. Everything changed, but the concept of the Barter system still going strong. I will give you love and compassion and expecting friendship from you. Everything has its own price. Living in this jungle among the bests and get motivated or inspired would be a mammoth task.

So my point is, if you need to build a strong self-belief don't depend on any one or don't listen to anyone.

It reminds me of a story. In a village a group of children were playing in a river. Suddenly a flash flood hit the river and water started rising fast. Everyone managed to reach the shore. But one boy stuck up in the rock in the middle of the river. By seeing the fast flowing water, no one dare to dive in water and rescue him.

Suddenly one boy from the group who was deaf by birth, jumps into the water. With all his strength he managed to swim towards the rock and managed to rescue the boy.

Can you tell me, how the boy managed to throw himself in such a dangerous situation and save his friend. Many answers are coming your mind. Right.

Answer is simple. This deaf boy, in his entire life time didn't hear any of the below comments from anyone that You can't do it, you are just a kid, you don't have the strength to do it, it's not your cup of tea, you are weak, you don't have the capacity to do it, you have many limitations, take care of yourself and don't help others etc.

His deafness has become his power. Now more than his limitations he knows the possibilities and strength he has. He will experience the unlimited power he holds. We all hold the same power, but the above statements have built a strong boundary around us and reduced our powers to a great extent.

So, if you want to unleash the power of self-belief, then be deaf towards the world and believe in yourself. Look at yourself not from the point of view of the world but with the inner eye. You will see the Super hero.

Next point is that, whenever you find yourself in adverse situation, don't panic or don't lose hope thinking that the world or the god is acting against me. Your character is built on how you act upon each situation. These situations can built or break your self-belief. If you think a negative situation as negative then it's negative. But if you try to find some positive elements in it then it would be an entire different situation you are in and you won't complain to others or put the responsibility of the situation of others.

One story which I would like to share with you. There was a single mother who had a cute baby. She had gone through an operation and on complete bed rest. Due to the high dosage of medicine she is not able to stand or walk.

Her baby was playing on a nearby construction site and the baby felt from the first floor of the site and bleeding badly. She heard the voice and ran outside and she had the worst shock of her lifetime. She didn't find any vehicle to take her to hospital. So she took her baby and ran to the hospital which was around one or two kilometres from her home. She was crying loudly and running. Reached hospital and doctors took the baby to causality and ask her to wait outside.

She was crying and cursing god. That I haven't done anything wrong till now. Always came to your temple and do all the rituals without asking anything and why are you giving all the pains to me. She was very angry with the god. Her full body was shivering that time also.

After a while, doctor came to her and told that the boy is perfectly fine. Have some wounds and nothing more. We have given some medicine and injections and he is sleeping. You can take him once he is awake. For her it was like a rebirth. She was so happy and sat on the chair still crying. After some times, she just rewind the incident and she understand that it was not the gods plan to destroy her.

She thought that. For two days, I am lying on bed and not able to walk or sit for a minute but just now I ran one or two kilometre holding the baby and I don't feel the pain and weakness. The construction site had iron rods, bricks and rocks which the construction labours cleared in the morning. If it's not removed then my baby will fall on it and it would be an entire different situation. Then she understands the biggest lesson of her life time, if god test you then he will give you the power also to withstand the test. We only like to see the negative side of his test. We always forget to see his hands which is holding us in the darkest path. We get scared and think that he pushed us to the darkness, but he won't leave us alone in the darkness. When we start walking in the darkness, he will be behind us to make sure we are safe.

So any adverse situation handle it with positive mind set and it's always good to believe and trust the super natural power. You can call it by any name. It's this belief , which keeps us alive. So always believe that, you are not alone. These believes can change your belief system and gives you power and energy to face any situation. Once our belief system is too strong than no one in the entire world can destroy us. It would be like "the more you beat me the more stronger I will become" . I can't be stopped or paused by anyone. I decide where to start, how to start and find a reason why to start. That should be extent of my will power. Its un matched in this world.

No matter, who believes in you or who care for you or who stand for you, the vital point is that do you believe in yourself. Do you trust your ability or do you trust yourself, your judgement and your competencies. If yes, then automatically you will be having the feeling of Self-respect.

These two traits of Confidence and belief will play a major part in improving your self-respect. Unless and until I respect myself, nothing matters. I have everything but I don't find a reason why I should respect myself. Then having everything in the world will not make any difference in your life. Self-respect should come from within you. It's your attitude.

There are many animals in jungle. But we all with same voice voted Lion as the king of the jungle. Lion is not the strongest animal or the fastest or the most dangerous animal of Jungle. There are many other animals who are much better than Lion and who have the proficiency to be the king of jungle. But still Lion holds this position for a very long time.

It's because of its belief. It's his belief and its belief is so strong that it transformed itself from just an ordinary animal to the king of the jungle. It has transformed its habit, attitude, ego and everything from ordinary to royal.

What you are currently is just a matter of time. But what you believe you will make a big difference. It can lift you up to the sky or it can drop you to the bottom crust of earth.

Tiger goes two steps back to take a big jump to catch it's pray. When it goes back, everyone think that it has quit and leaves the game. But to everyone's surprise it takes the biggest jump from there.

When your time is not favouring you, take two steps back and wait till your prey comes to your radar. It takes some time, be patience and close your ears and mind towards the world as you may hear many negative comments or humiliation and believe in yourself. Keep your senses and eyes wide open. Once you feel, it's the time. Take the biggest jump with all the strength and vitality you have.

Then the world understands the tiger didn't quit the game. It was waiting for its opportunity and once the opportunity showed its sign then history has been created.

We respect those people, whom we feel that they have some skills or competencies which we lack or we don't have.

Respect can be of two type. You respect a leader because of his influence he had towards the community. That's the respect earned. Other is you don't respect the leader but respect the position he or she hold or the chair he or she is sitting. Once he don't have the position your respect towards the person will be minimum.

I always tell to my team that, the best appreciation you can get is not the Best Employee award or an appreciation email from your Manager coping everyone in the organisation or getting rewards and recognition. The best appreciation is the seeing the respect in the eyes and words of your supervisor. That's the respect which comes directly from the bottom of heart and it's the purest form of appreciation and it's earned with your hard work and sweat. Respect can't be get by paying money or by any other way. You have to work hard and earn it. When you join an organisation, everyone's attitude towards you will be just normal or as usual. But over these years, with your skills and with your hard and smart work you change the your image in the organisation or in the society and then see the way your colleagues, client, Manager management or the people around you speak to you or look at you. You can see the respect in their eyes. You can feel the difference. These will make you feel that you are not an ordinary asset and the moment you start feel that you are not ordinary, then it will increase your self-respect and it will motivate you to go beyond your limits and try to explore all the possibilities which is available.

These appreciations and recognitions are like a addictions. Once you start getting these it will boost up your confidence and self-reliance. Once you get the respect in the team or organisation then you will feel to have more and more of it. Once you get more, there will be a situation where you can't live without recognitions or respect. Believe me, it hold so much power. We have seen politicians who once elected to power will always want to be in power till the last moment of their life. They have seen the power of respect and now they can't even think of living without it.

It's only the matter of tasting your first success. If you taste your first success then you will go to any limits to get it again and once you get it again then your mind accepted that this as the greatest feeling you can ever have and it will start working for it harder and harder to get it again.

A Lion's cub accepts the fact that he is just a kid unless it tastes the first drop of fresh blood and flesh. Once it tastes, then it understand that it is not just an another animal and he is meant to rule the Jungle as a king. Once it understands its strength and calibre then no one can stop it. So work hard for the first fresh blood and flesh. Once you get it you will be transformed to an entire different person with no time.

There is a saying in Urdu. Make yourself so big and huge with your work that when god is writing your destiny. He will ask us. Tell me, what I should write for you. "*Khud ko itna kar buland ki har taqdeer sa pahala khuda banda sa pucha, batha banda teri raza kya hai*"

Now the question raises is how to get the appreciation and recognition. It's not something which you can buy in market or you will get in charity.

If you are working in an organisation, you might have seen many teams who are competing with each other to be the Best team. Or there are members inside your team competing with each other for the Best member of the team. Then the best way to start is, identify the best team or the best individual in your team and compete with them. Always compete with the first or the best team. Don't ever compromise on that. With a small example I want to prove my point.

In cricket we know, India is always among the best three cricketing country in the world. Suppose an underdog team like Hongkong, UAE, Oman or Nepal who are now taking baby steps in International cricket can't dream of defeating India. If any of these team play a series of three matches then Team India will brutally defeat them without any mercy. But suppose the same team is having a series of thirty matches with India. Then we can easily notice that the margin of defeat in the 30th match will be much lower than the margin of defeat in the first match. You never know, these underdogs might won any of the last five matches too.

After the tournament, if they face any other teams in the world they will have a good chance of winning. It's because playing with the best team in the world. They have gone through the toughest challenge and all the players had struggled to a great extent, they understand the strategy which the best team has taken against them. They know the strength of the best team. They know the weakness of the best team. They know each best players calibre and potential. They know how best bowlers ball in each pitch condition. They know how the best batters shot selection. The best teams field settings and its strategy based on the bowling attack. At spin bowling how they set the field on pace bowling how they set the filed. In short, they know each and everything about the best team of the world. If they adopt these techniques and strategies. Sooner or later they have a high chance of being the best team.

That's why I was telling; only compete with the best team. If you are competing with a medium team then again you have left with option to reach only to the second position as the best team will still holds its first position. While competing with any team, we always try to think like them, act like them and make plans and strategies like them. These slowly become the part of our habit. So while trying to shadow any one or any team. Make sure that you are shadowing the best team in the Industry.

An example is that. If you follow Chateshwar Pujara's batting style in test cricket then there is high chance of reaching to the top three batters. But if you are following him for T20 or IPL then you are in big danger. So it's very important who are following or shadowing. If your selection is wrong then all your efforts will go in vain.

Next point is about sweet revenge. Which I would like to call it. We get lots of negative feedback. From supervisor, from parents, from peers or even from our friends. We know that they are correct but its human tendency not to accept or agree on any negative comments. As its said that we react in three ways on negative comments. Fight, Flight or Freeze.

We will Fight, if we get the negative comments or we would like to leave the room or end the conversation sooner which is called Flight or we will Freeze our self when someone is giving negative comments or we will fight by giving justification of those situation which we also know it's not true.

Just imagine, instead of these. If we accept the fact that I have some weak areas and it can be improved. If I take this negative comments on positive way then work hard to rectify or overcome it and give a mission statement to our self that, the same person who had given me the negative comment should appreciate me for the same act. That would be the sweetest revenge we can ever have. It sound harsh, as I am using the word revenge. But just remember one thing. As I mentioned earlier, this is a Jungle and if you want to survive and be the best then we have to be more brutal than others. You have to be harsh sometime. There is nothing wrong in that. If you are soft, then others will attack and demolish you without any mercy. So keep my space and my dignity, I can go to any extend. Everything is fair in love and war and we are in the battle field where there is minimum love an maximum war and expecting the worse.

Fight hard and be the greatest warrior the world have ever seen, who fought the intense battle not with the lethal weapons but with determination, motivation and the passion of dreams and made all the heads bowed in front of him. Are you seeing the warrior in the mirror? If not, then your passion and determination has not reached to the level. Long way to go, but surely will reach to the level where when you see the mirror, you should feel the traits of the greatest warrior.

One thing I want to share with you. I completed by Graduation in Nagpur. On those days, on every vacation I used to travel to Kerala which is my home land in Train. I always booked my train ticket in KK Express. If the ticket is not available, I would wait for days but always make sure that I travel only in that train. Not because it's the only train or the best train. Of course it was the best train.

Most of the Army men used that train to travel from Delhi. I love to talk to them and hear their stories, which always fascinate me a lot. One of the soldier told me about the commando training. Commando training are the most intense training in Indian Army. Where they will make sure that you see all the places and pains of hell. Army jawans join the Commando trainings not for any hike in salary or for any materialistic gains or for any other perks. They will get a medal which they put in their uniform with pride and any Army person who carries this medal will get the most respect across the Indian Army camps and barracks. Just imagine all these pains for a medal. That's the power of respect.

Can't share a better example of self-respect than this. I sometimes think, what kind of bread are these Army men. Army training is like transforming soft cotton to the hardest steel. Really hats off and god bless them for everything they do to our country.

It doesn't require any effort to live an ordinary life. Just live the life as it is. It's like a piece of wood floating in the water. Which all direction the water moves without any resistance or struggle the wood will go along with water. It doesn't have any destiny of its own. The woods destiny will be completely depend on the waters destiny. We are going where ever life is taking us. No struggle, no resistance, no dream no passion nothing. Only at the end of life we understand what is our destiny.

Life is all about a journey from ordinary to extra ordinary. For those who think, that there is nothing in me or I don't have any quality, which I can respect or believe I am extra ordinary. I am just an another creation of God. Where god created me on his holiday or his day off. For those who thinks like that I just want to tell you one thing.

Have you gone to a Super speciality hospital and look at the departments on the board in reception. ENT, Orthopaedic, Neurologist, Dermatologist, Pulmonologist, Dentist, Cardiologist, Heart specialist, Physician, Oncologist, Eye Doctors and many more.

Have you ever wondered, for an ordinary body and brain there are so much of departments and so much variety of doctors. These are the doctor who have the best brains in the country or in the world who requires four to seven years to complete the study of one part of body and medical science has not completed the study of the human body till now. Still research are going and daily they are finding new things about the body and brains.

If I talk about our brain, it would take an another million years for medical fraternity to study it completely. Still not sure. If it can be studied completely with this time period.

So just imagine, are we really and ordinary human being. From a single cell, we reached to a community of millions and trillion cells and if we still think that we are an ordinary person in this world then we need some consultation. My finger prints to my face, everything is unique. Just imagine, if nature has put these much of effort on me and given all my organs in very good working condition and we are not doing justice to the creation, then it's a big sin we are committing towards the nature and purpose of our creation.

God is like a financer or a start-up company promoter who had financed or sponsored everything we need to start the business and he is just asking us to put your whole hearted effort and we are making stupid excuses. What else can you ask to god.

Our ancestors who lived in Stone Age where great fighters. To survive they had to fight to the core. They had taken pain and fight hard. With nature with wild with beasts and with themselves. If they have thought the same and quit the fight then human race would had not been existed by now. They had fought and fought hard and killed in the fight. That's the only reasons we are here. We are the descended of those fighters and we also have the same traits and DNA which they had. Only difference is that. They were forcefully put to the situation where they don't have any option other than to fight for their existence. But we have option. To fight or not to fight and we have selected the most convenient option of not to fight. So if I am looser then I only hold the responsibility for it, not anyone else.

On a daily basis, we should improve and improvise our self. As it's human nature to reject anything which is not improved or changed. We don't give much importance to those things or people who shows reluctant to change.

Many years back, if someone had gifted you with a Nokia 3310 mobile. You will jump with joy as at that time it was the hot cake in town. Everyone wants the own the beauty. But now, if anyone gift you the same phone. We throw it away without opening its cover. It's because, when everyone and everything had changed and the phone was stagnant and didn't change. So we lost the interest or respect towards the mobile.

Same way, if we don't change or improve yourself. You will lose respect towards you. Always do something new or learn something new. Push yourself, push hard and ready to take the pain. The more pain you take the more gain you will have.

One short story I would like to tell related this topic. One day a Sculpture who create beautiful stone carvings is passing through a jungle. Where he found two stones. He liked both the stones and want to make a statue of God with it. So to take permission he approached the first stone and asked the stone. I would like to make a statue of God with you can I go ahead.

The stone told that, please don't do it. As you will beat me with the hammer in the process of making statue, I will be having pain. So please leave me. Sculpture approached the second stone and asked the same question. Which the stone agreed to it. Sculpture told that it's a painful process. Are you sure you want to do it. The stone told, it's fine with me. You can go ahead.

He brought all his tools and started making the statue. In the process as Sculpture told. The stone has to go through tremendous pain. But the stone without shouting or crying handled the pain.

After sometime, the stone turned to a beautiful statue of God and later it was kept on a temple and the other stone who was afraid of pain, was kept just outside the temple where people break coconut on it.

The moral of the story is that, the stone who was ready to take all the pain is worshiped as god and seen with immense respect and the stone who want to run away from pain has to undergo tremendous pain of coconut each and every minute.

So be open to changes. Open your mind and all sense and accept all good changes and acquire more and more skills and information and always make sure that your current day is not exactly same as your previous day. If it's the same, then you are in a trouble. On daily basis learn something new and do something new and make sure your daily life is not a carbon copy of yesterday.

Always be hungry and thirsty. Make sure that your hunger or thirst never dies. What all or how much you in take, your hunger or thirst should never die. I have heard stories of people who lost in Desert and when the thirst hit its upper limit and you know there is no way you will get water. Then you will think of drinking urinal. Sounds weird, right. It's fact. To survive we can go to any extend. We can eat raw meat by killing animals. Just to keep us alive. Suppose, if we have the same level of hunger and thirst in us then imagine what all it can do to us.

It can take us to an entire different world. Always keep hunger and thirst to its upper limit and what all and how much you get should not satisfy your hunger and thirst to a single percentage. Then your life will be an entire different ball game.

It's not a rocket science. Equation is very simple. you know what you have and you know what you want. Then you have to just build a bridge between the two points. It's not as complicated as it looks like. Only complication here is to understand both the points. It may take little effort, but once you understand both the points of what you have and what you want then the game begin.

In this game there won't be any umpire or referee. You set the rules, you change the rule and you have every right to break the rule. In short, it's your game and no one will interfere or don't allow anyone to interfere. Play hard and play tight. Winning is not the destiny or your target. Keeping the game alive should be the prime target. Focus on the game not the result.

Have you ever climbed mountain or a hill? If you are climbing seeing the steepness of the hill or mountain. You will be tired or exhausted soon. But if you are climbing by keeping your heads down and watching your steps then you can climb much easier. Here we are not looking at the big mountain or hill or the path we have to cover. We are only looking at the steps we are currently taking to reach at the top. So don't look at the final result which may look like a monster to you now. Only concentrate on the steps. Always tell yourself that it's not the kilometres that we have to go. It should always be about the meters that we have completed. These will bring the positive sense in you and use these positive vibe or senses to continue the rest of the climb.

There will be points where you will be stuck up and don't know how to get out of it. This is the point where many of us quit the game or start thinking that this game was not meant for me. Here we have to use our analytical or problem solving ability. We all have the skill to solve problem. But we are not able to solve the problem is just because we don't understand the problem completely. Before understanding the problem we start to work for solutions or we will pass our verdict about the problem and its solutions. Which will be absolute wrong.

Suppose your child had failed or got less grade in exams. As a parent we will only look at the total percentage and total marks first and start shouting at the child. Next time also for sure the same child will get the same score and it repeat.

Instead of that, understand the problem. Go step by step backward. Total score is less. On that how much subject he got good score and how much subject he got average and how much subject he got bad or worse score.

Make it three priorities. Bad score subjects are on first priority. Need to evaluate it quickly. Average score subjects can wait but still can't wait for long time. Good score subjects can wait.

Suppose he got lowest score in Maths. Then take his answer sheet and look which all questions he went wrong. By that you can understand which all topics he is week or he doesn't understand. Which all topic he got full marks then can be second priority. Concentrate on the weaker topics and make him understand the concept. It may take time but it will happen. Then look on the other topics. Once you done the full evaluation of all subject and prepare a Time table based on that. Do you think your child will fail again?

Instead of shouting or screaming, understand the situation completely. Do a proper analysis and make a game plan. Instead of putting the tag of a failure to your child's forehead this will be a better option right. What do you think?

Most of the complex or big problems have simple solutions. Only think is that we have to dissect the problems in parts and analysis it separately. Same as how an autopsy is done.

In a museum in US. There was a big statue of Abraham Lincoln surrounded by flood light and it has to be clean with high concentrate chemicals due to birds and insects shit. These chemicals are affecting the texture and the quality of status. So everyone was thinking what to do. After lot of meeting they understand the problem. Flood lights where switched on just before sun set and it was noticed that the insects and birds are attracted towards the light and they came and sit on the statue and shit on the statue. So the museum staffs decided to switch on the light after sun set and noticed that the insects and birds population near the statue has dropped tremendous and in long run the statue was not much spoiled and frequency of cleaning the statue reduced a lot.

So the point is that for any complex problem, if you diagnosis the situation or the problem by considering its all angles then you will reach to a solution which would be very simple when compared with the problem. All it need is to understand the problem in its correct sense then you will reach to its root case.

There was a factory which has a single production line. Means from raw material to finished goods it processed in a single production line. It's like a single machine which has different subsets and everything is connected with each other. One day the machine break down and the entire production of the factory stopped. It raised panic in all departments as entire production is stopped and if it's not started soon then company may have to face huge loss. Each and every seconds count. Top engineers came and checked. They analysed all possible causes for the break down. But after long time they have given up. They were not able to find the root cause of the issue. Company hired services from other professional groups to resolve the issue. They too failed. Tension was raising to its peak. The local plumber came to the production floor and he asked the floor manager "Can I check the machine". The floor manager who was overwhelmed with tension first didn't mind. Again the plumber asked the same question. He got angry with the plumber. Said the big engineers were not able to identify the issue. What can you do. Plumber said to give one chance to check the machine. Manager given the permission. Plumber with his hammer slowly hitting the part of the machine and was walking by looking at the machine. After sometime he stopped at a point and watched the machine for some time and with all the force he hit the hammer on the machine. To everyone's surprise the machine started working. Within a second the news spread like a wild fire across all departments and everyone came to see the plumber and to congratulate him.

Manager asked plumber how much will you charge for this service. Plumber said, My charges would be $1,000. Manager was shocked to hear it. $1,000 for just banging the hammer. Are you joking or what. Then plumber told. To bang the hammer I will only charge $10. Rest $990 is to find the right point to bang the hammer. It's as simple as that.

So once you have a problem then with all your experience and analytical skills its necessary to identify the problem. Then break it into small pieces and then identify the spot to bang the hammer.

It's not about what you do. It's always about how you do. Just imagine in an organisation you work for three, five or ten years and you resign. Within a week time a new member will take your position and he or she will be trained on all your tasks and start working on it. Within a week or less than that your colleagues, managers and the company will forget you. No trace of your existence will be left in the organisation or in your team.

Just imagine, is there anything bad than this could ever happen to you. You have dedicated your time and energy to the company and within a week or little more than that your existence is vaporised without leaving a trace. I don't know how you will justify the situation. If you ask me, I would say without any doubt that my x number of years in the organisation is wasted. If my position can be easily replaced in a week time then what's my value.

My value is not more than five or ten working days. 10 years of my working in a company can be replaced in five or ten working days.

You can't always shout to the world and say you exist. Your work should shout it out. If you give more than what is expected from you on daily basis, then you can feel the difference. Instantly you might not get any rewards or recognition. The time you put the resignation letter, it will press the panic button. From your colleagues to the management will be on panic mode. Once you resign and get out of the office. Your position can be replaced but your space and the value you build over the years will never go down or it can't be replaced easily. For a long time you will be remembered in the company. As I said earlier. Don't do many things, Do handful things which you are the best. Improve your skill sets and knowledge on daily basis and see the difference.

As its said. If you had given an axe to cut a big tree in five hours. Spend one to two hours in sharpening the axe and use the other three hours to cut it. You will cut the tree more effectively with high productivity and without wasting much time.

In personal life or in professional life excel your skills. Your skill is your weapon by which you will recognise or identified with. Your name and what all you make in this life will perish and no one will remember it. But the skill you have will always been remembered for ever. So make sure make your skills the most dangerous and leather weapon. So that if you are there or not. You will always live in the mind and heart of others.

Just a last point before I conclude the topic. I know I am dragging this topic too much. For that I want to ask apology. As I have many things to tell to you. What all comes to my mind. I am writing. Hope you can understand. I don't want to leave no stone unturned.

We Indian's like to drag situations very much. That's why our Indian family serials are super hit across India. Where the heroine of the serial become pregnant and after two years delivery will happen. We all know it, it will drag to the core. But still we never miss a single episode.

We all are part of many games. In personal life and professional life. Like the company we are working, has designed a game and we are part of the game. We have been assigned the script and role to play on the game. Same like our family is like a game. Where every member has to play his part in the game. From childhood days we have been taught only to look for our part in the game. No need to understand anything else. So we are only interested to know what is my part in the game. We put our effort to justify our part. Once my part is completed then I am relaxed. We seldom care about the rest.

We should change our mind set a little bit. Instead of just knowing my part of the game. How about understanding the game completely. From end to end. Like, who designed this game, who all are the participants and who hold the most power in this game, who is the referee of the game, does the role played by me have any significance in the game or how critical is it. What is actually expected from my role and what I am delivering? Who is the weakest link in the game and who is the strongest link. Get all possible information about the game. Then you will have a clear visibility of what's happening or you will know the entire story. A holistic or an Arial view of the game. You can quantify your role and can improve as it's needed in game. You can extend your services to others. Then you will clearly understand the opportunities lying in front of you.

It's important to understand that the game you in is relevant in the current scenario and always flexible to change the rules or change the game as and when required. For example, many years back Typewriters where booming and if we are in the game of typewriters and happy with playing our part of the game. Then we won't be realising that the entire game would be over when Computers hit the market. One fine morning we realise that the game we are in doesn't even exist and we are in a situation where we don't know what to do next. So always monitor the entire game from an aerial route and understand the threats in advance so that you can make changes well before it hit you. Be proactive than reactive. Always be on toes.

Don't just be products of a single game. Understand the game and grab all the opportunities which comes to your way. If you are just concentrating on Test cricket and suppose one day ICC declare that they are stopping all the Test series due to its declining popularity then you will be out of business. Instead of that, if you are constantly monitoring the entire game then you would realise the trend is changing and you would adopt yourself to T20 and One day much earlier than ICC stop Test cricket. So don't be adamant be flexible. If you feel that the boat you are sailing is sinking then find the best option . Do you want to sink or swim .

If you are just interested in playing your role only then you are like a frog in the well. Who thinks that world will start and end in the well.

So change your mind set or rather open your mind and understand the game completely. Then you will be a resource who can be fit to any game.

So to conclude this topic. Find your game. Once you find your game then put all your effort and energy to a single point, which will bring confidence and self-belief and in long run which will in turn brings respect to your life and will change the face of your life. Transformation from Black and white television to a 4K HD 60 Inch TV.

Understand one thing. It's the survival of fittest and if you play the game on the mercy of others or if you play the game on rules , terms and conditions of others then also you are killing the purpose of the game. This game is for you and you have to play by creating your rules, break the existing rule, do all the experiments to find the winning combinations. Always make sure that you can provide full justice to it.

A life without self-respect is like a death by thousand cut. Daily you will be crushed and cornered by any Tom Dick and Harry. So it's all about finding a space and value for yourself in this jungle.

Get connected to the nature

This will be the last topic of my book but definitely not the least important topic. What all we achieve in life what all we have in life is irrelevant if we are not connected to nature.

We have millions of money in bank and we have all the comfort in the world .We can buy anything which money can buy. But, if we have Diabetics or Sugar or any chronic diseases then what will we do with all these money. You have a chocolate factory but you can't eat a single piece of chocolate. You are running a hotel chain but you can't eat any dish. It's like the sailor who is stuck in the island in between ocean and cries. Water, water everywhere but not a drop to drink.

Have you ever noticed, what all we requires, nature gives us. All the vitamins minerals protein and all the minute supplement which body require comes from nature in form of fruits, vegetables, grains etc. Which means we are the part of nature. Our body and mind is the child of our mother nature and the mother nature always enrich us with everything we need. But what are we doing. We always try to separate the child from the mother.

We have a ton of excuses for it. Don't have time, busy schedule, where will nature goes. I will retire and then I will enjoy and be with nature now I don't have time etc. The more you go away from the nature the more miserable our life will become. We haven't realised the power of our mother nature. It seems so calm and quite, hence we have taken it as granted.

Many people lived in the planet earth got enlightenment by connecting with this nature. Nature has the answer to our all unsolved questions, miseries and sorrows. Only thing is that we should stop identifying our-self different from nature. We should connect with nature. It's like the Bluetooth connecting devices. To connect with Bluetooth you just have to On the Bluetooth on the device and it will be connected. Just like that open your senses and mind and we will be connected to the nature.

In today's competitive world, being introvert is not considered as a good idea. But unless I know myself how can I connect with nature. I should connect to nature as I am from inside. That would be the purest form of connection which I can establish with the nature. Then Nature will answer all my questions, including the million dollar question "Who am I?". Which we all are trying to find the answer for our entire life. Once you know or understand yourself, then only you have the option to explore yourself. Once you explore yourself then only you can discover more and more characteristics, abilities and calibre in you. The more you understand these traits the more you will use it. More you use it, the more stronger you will be. More stronger you will be the more deeper the connection will be. More deeper the connection, you will explore much more about you. It's a cycle which will constantly take you to different levels which you never dream of. It's not about finding the limits in you. It's all about identifying yourself beyond the limits.

We have seen our Grandparents and their generation. They are so connected to nature. They walk bare foot and wake up early in the morning and they always make sure to spend quality time outside. They always engage themselves by doing some or other work. At age of 80's and 90's they can easily walk four to five kilometres. They don't expect any comfort zone in their life. They don't have TV or smart phones to kill their time. They were productive for the entire day.

But now, we have everything in our finger tips. Life is change and living standards also changed. We call it an improved living standard compared to earlier generations. An improved living standard where we don't have fresh air, don't have fresh food, don't have a healthy body, can't climb 10 stairs, running from pharmacy to pharmacy for medicines. Regardless of all the vitamins, protein, iron etc which nature gives us in abundance, we still count on Multi vitamin tablets and supplement medicine. Going to Yoga classes and gym to make ourselves fit but our body fat don't want to go away.

On a radius of one kilometre there are at least two hospitals or clinics who are making decent money from us. We are so busy in making money which we have to spend in hospital. Still we advocate for the life style we live in and we consider the village population as second category citizens of our country who lives with nature. That's the irony, we think we have everything but the matter of fact is that we don't have anything.

Have we ever realised, even though we don't care about the nature but our mother nature always care about us. Nature is working day in day out to feed us. It has assigned farmers for us to make sure that we don't sleep in hunger. It has planted trees for you and me, so that we don't have to struggle for oxygen. When we get exhausted in summer, it will give a nice heavy summer rain in between and change the climate, so that we can relax and start again. How hot be the afternoon is, you will always find a tree, under which you can sit and relax. Divided all seasons equally, so that we don't have struggle much. Even though, we don't care about her. She will care each and every one without expecting anything.

We are searching god everywhere. In temples, mosques churches etc. We believe that God created this world and it's taking care of everything. It's a supreme power. Which we haven't seen or experienced. Just imagine, in a summer afternoon when you are walking on road full of sweat and with no energy. A cold wind touches your body and make you feel energise. Can't that be the God's touch. When you are sitting demotivated and dejected and see the small bird building a nest just with its beak. Can't it be a sign from God to asking you to walk up and start again. "if a small bird can do with its beak, then why can't you do with your perfectly working body and mind". it's the nature who has taken utmost care to build us from a single cell to what we are now. Can't it be the God? It's the nature who had given us the immunity power, which fight all the bacteria and virus and protect us. Can't it be God? It's the nature who had given us emotions by which we can express ourselves. Can't it be God? It's the nature, who protects the womb of the mother for ten months. Can't it be God? It's the nature who helps to heal all the pains and sorrow. Can't it be God? It's the nature, who give the power to clout the blood after bleeding. Can't it be God? It's the nature who gives us power to raise after a big fall. Can't it be God? From childhood days it's the nature who teaches us. Life is not about running and winning. It's about running, falling falling falling falling and winning. Can't it be God? It's the nature who give light after darkness. Can't it be God? It's the nature who gives us the spectacular views of mountains, lakes, sea and much more and made our mind heart and soul rejuvenate with joy. Can't it be God? It's the nature who had given us the most complex organ in the world called Brain. By which human race become the most powerful species in this world. Can't it be God? It has given all the sensory organs by which we enjoy every aspect of life. Can't it be God? Nature has given taste buds by which we are enjoying our food. Can't it be God?

There are many to write, but I am stopping it here. It's said that, no one has ever seen God. But I would say, we are seeing and feeling God on every moment. But we are not realising.

When its rain, we would like to close our windows and door and like to sit inside. If we are outside we will curse nature. When was the last time we have enjoyed rain or played in rain or when was the last time you try to catch rain drop in hand? I bet, you may be putting immense pressure on brain to think that moment. My point is that, enjoy what nature wants to show you or want to give you. Fell the nature. Fell the rain, feel the wind and feel the sunshine. For sometimes remove all the boundaries which is between you and nature and sync with nature and then you will feel the difference. It would like, you are confronted with the supreme power. Doctor's even advice, new born babies to be exposed to rising sun which has Vitamin D and it will boost immunity.

Its highly recommended to start the day with Meditation, which can recharge your body and mind and electrify your entire system. I am telling this because, I am doing it for years and experiencing the difference. There are many methods of doing meditation which you will get. I will just narrate my way of doing it. I am not endorsing it or claim it as the correct or only method.

Sit on a peaceful place on the ground. Close your eyes and just be clam and inhale and exhale. Slowly try to reach to a state of vacuum, where there is no thoughts and no consciousness. When you start doing it, it would be difficult to control your thoughts, as our mind is so rebellious. If we try to control it will act against it. If you do it forcefully then we will never be able to control it.

I will give you an example. I will tell you a dish and for thirty seconds you should not think or imagine that dish in your thoughts. Nothing related to the dish should come to your mind.

Ready. Can I tell you. **Crispy Ghee Dosa with Coconut chatney and Sambar**. Look at the watch and from now till thirty seconds, don't think of Dosa, Chatey or Sambar. How is it. Hope are not thinking of Yammy Dosa. If I said just Ghee Dosa and all and didn't put the condition for not thinking for half a minute. Then you might have not thought of it. But when I said it. Then defiantly our mind will think about it.

So to control our thoughts, it require some time. Many people sitting on meditation and after one week, quitting it as they can't see any difference. It's a gradual process. It take time and patience. To control your thoughts and to reach the state of mind is not that easy but it's not impossible.

I can put more light on this point with a small example. Suppose you go with your small naughty kid to a Shopping Mall. If you don't have kids, don't get upset. You can imagine it's your neighbours kid or any of your family members kid. On the Shopping Mall there is a big session for Toys. Your naughty kid sees the toy session and you are holding your kids hand and telling the kid not to go. He is not listening. Then you started shouting at the kid. Still the kid not giving ears to you. Kid starting crying, screaming and started biting, hitting and scratching your body. At any cost the kid want to go to the Toy session and at any cost you won't allow the kid to go to the Toy session. After a while the situation will be totally mess up. You starting beating the kid and with full of frustration you will leave the shopping mall and will make sure that you will never come back to the Mall with the kid.

That's what happen with most of us while trying to meditate. Our mind is like the small kid. It doesn't want to be under control and it want to explore the Toy session and we are trying to control it. It became more fierce and we are stubborn to control it. Then you killed the purpose. The mind or brain which you want to control is getting out of control and you can't do anything. Instead of getting peace and silence you are creating a war like situation. It won't work that way.

Now take the same situation. You and the kid are standing near to the Toy session and the kid want to go to the Toy session. You leave the kids hand and allow him to go to the Toy session. You sit on a bench near to the Toy session and watch the kid play with toys. What all he do, which all toys he is playing, how is playing and which toys attract him and all. Don't use much of the brain or logic. Just watch the kid play and cherish the moment when your kid is enjoying and smiling. In between the kid look at you to make sure that you are there and after confirming your presence again continue playing. The kid is very much happy and his energy level is sky high. Kid is living one of the happiest moment in his life. It may take one hour, two hour or five or might be little more than that, when your kid will be tired and bored of playing with the toy . He will come back to you with all gratitude and love will hug you and then the kid will be more obedient then before because you waited and didn't disturbed the kid when he was living his dream on the Toy shop.

Same way our mind too works. When sitting for meditation. Let free your mind. Let it go anywhere it wants. Let it show any picture it want to show. Let it enjoy itself. Just wait and watch all those which mind want to show it to you. Just enjoy the moment. Don't think that you are on a mission called meditation. Be with yourself. After some time, our mind slowly comes to our control. It will be claim and quiet. That's the moment you start experience the magic of meditation. It will lead you to the next level. Where there are no thoughts or no emotions and no identification of me or you. It would be like sitting in a black hole which doesn't have a start or end point.

In short, our brain or mind who works 24/7 by generating thoughts when we are awake or asleep will be calm. In simple words, a machine which works for 24/7 for many years will not give optimum productivity, as somehow some where it will be tired. By doing this process, we are re starting the machine or giving it a break for some time and then once it restart then it will work at much high capacity than we expect. Its power will be unimaginable and unmatched. It can do wonders in your life by reducing your tension, anxiety, increases your decision taking capacity, look at the issues from a different point of view, improves sleep, decrease many body issues, improves attention and concentration and improves our emotional health and many more advantages it has.

It brings a solid connection with the nature or what we called supreme power. It has the power to change you completely. By doing medication you can easily reduce your sleep time. I am telling it with my experience and it's against what science says. As I mention earlier, it's my point of view.

Science says, our body need 7 to 8 hours of sleep a day. But I personally don't agree with it. For those who are working in office or most of the population who are not much involved in physical activities didn't use much energy in a day. Most of us are sitting in a comfortable chair and working and do minimum physical activities to get tired. If I stand for half an hour in a lane and sit for ten minute my body will regain the energy it lost while standing. I don't need to sleep to regain the energy. If I work physically for two to three hour and take rest for half an hour then again my energy level will be back to normal, definitely a little energy will be lost on this . By considering these cases, at end of the day why I should require 7 to 8 hours of sleep. When I didn't done anything much in a day to get tired. Only thing, if I eat a lot. My body need to work with extra energy and extra time to digest it. Then it requires some rest. But if I eat only what I require and do my regular task with regular breaks then I can manage with 4 hours of sleep. Rest for the brain and our mind who works 24 hours a day, I can rejuvenate by performing medication.

Suppose you have a machine which you bought it by paying a huge amount and imagine you have to feed the machine for four to five times a day and give rest to the machine for 7 to 8 hours a day. You have to give frequent breaks. Like Meal break, tea break, coffee break, lunch break, restroom break, smoking break and many other breaks and the machine will not work on weekends and holidays. On daily the break time can increase by reducing the work time. Work time can't be increased by compromising break time. This machine will have issues regarding mood swings, emotion issues, office politics, watch cricket, gossips and chit chat etc which again eat productivity.

Now tell me, how many of you will dare to invest a big amount in a machine like this. This would be the most incompetent machine when compared to all other species in the world. Still we advocate for 7 to 8 hours of sleep. If you ask me. I would say, four hour of power nap and good quality time of meditation and light meals will give you so much energy which you can use it for entire day and believe me, some energy will be still left out or unused when you touch the bed for sleep at night.

So to end the topic, connect to the nature and always understand that without the supreme power called Mother Nature we are nothing. It takes some minute for the nature to convert a Boxing Day celebration venue to a graveyard in the form of Tsunami. If we live our life in sync with nature, our life will be high peace and harmony. Enjoy and feel each and every face of nature. Nature has managed the eco system in such a way that every species has its own space. When we try to step outside our border then the issue will start.

Now it's the time for me to say good bye. As I mentioned in the entire book, life is a simple game with simple rules. We are making it more complicated. We are trying to implement the rules of football in basketball and crying and cursing ourselves for not being a good player. First of all, sit alone, relax and try to understand the game and rules of the game. Once you understand the rule and know how the game is played. Then you will enjoy. It's like good lawyers always lean the law in and out. That's why they are good in finding the loopholes of the law. So first understand the rule of the game and play hard.

As now we both are connected through this book and by the time when you complete the book, not sure I might be alive or dead. But just understand one thing, everything in this world happens for a reason. You reading the book today might not be a coincident. You don't know, what the nature want to communicate with you. I am not telling you that this is the ultimate book. I am sure it's not. You will get a million times better book than this in market. It doesn't matter who is the Author of the book. What is his taste, politics or his feelings? What matter is, is there anything for me in the book. That's how you should see. If in this book, you only like one point. Accept the one point and reject the entire book.

Dronacharya in Mahabharat is a great Coach of all time. But he was not that great human. He killed the spirit of game by asking the thumb of the greatest Archer, who could have changed the history. But we have a lot to learn from Drona as a Teacher. That should be the only part we should be concerned. What I can get from Drona as a coach. If I get something what I require, make him your Guru. Don't look at any other aspect. It's irrelevant and no one is perfect. But everyone has a perfect aspect. Concentrate on that.

We have a habit of criticising a person as a whole. Don't do it. Criticise his or her negative side and appreciate the positive side. If you are impressed with the positive side, try to acquire it. Don't be judgemental.

With said that, If you can acquire a single point from this book, will satisfy my purpose of putting the effort to write the book. A small spark is enough to fire an entire forest and a small ray of light and hope is all it requires to enlighten yourself. A king called Sidhartha Gautama got the answer of the million dollar question "Who am I" and he became a religious Guru and worshiped as god.

Every human being born in this beautiful earth has a purpose to accomplish. To kill the most powerful ruler in Lanka it requires a king from Ayodhya which is in Uttar Pradesh, a city thousands of miles away from Lanka. But Ram accepted and followed the sequence of challenges thrown towards him and at last with a small ape army he killed the mightiest king his brothers and entire Lankan Army. Nature knows your destiny and when time comes, it will start putting situations in front of you and will force to form the sequence. Without knowing it. We will start connecting the dots and reach our destiny. A South Indian Boy becomes CEO of Google (Sundar Pichai), A Tea seller in Gujarat becomes the Prime Minister of India (Narandra Modi), A Bus conductor in Tamil Nadu becomes the Movie Super star (Rajanikanth), A boy from an average family with high dreams build an empire called Reliance (Dhirubhai Ambani) . From Watchman in Delhi to be a super actor in Bollywood (Nawazuddin Siddiqui). The boy who was rejected in the school Basketball team went to become the Ever Time Star of Basketball, (Michael Jordan). A Girl sexually abused at 9. Ran away from home at 13, pregnant at 14 is the first Black American women on National Television in America (Oprah Winfrey). A boy who is tagged as "stupid to learn anything" by teachers is the greatest scientist of all time. (Thomas Edison). These are some, there are many inspiring names in the list. Some follow the sequence and dots and many won't. That's why, success rate in the world is very low.

God had given challenges and on same note give opportunity too. When time comes nature or the supreme power will give signs and will arrange all the means to achieve it. You walk on the road of fire with bare foot and take all the pain which comes to you as a fuel to move ahead. When we fall on your back, don't look back. Continue walking. At any cost, don't look back.

Just remember one thing. God will write our story till half and leave the rest half for us to complete. It's us who decide how to complete the story. With golden ink or with normal.

There is only one or two page of pain left in your book. Then the history is created. So live the two or three pages of pain to the fullest. Enjoy the pain by dreaming about the success. Then the pain will not have the strength to pull you down.

Dreams are like fire balls which will fascinate when you watch it from a distance. But when you decide to jump towards the fire of dream. It will burn you from inside. It will make your life much worse than hell. You will scream and want to run away. It will break all your bones and make you stand. It will make you run bare foot on the sizzling hot road with winter cloths and a baggage of half a ton on your back. It will not let you sleep. It will take all your happiness and social life from you. It will make you isolated. On each and every step, it will test you to core. Still if you didn't give up and still you are in the fire ball.

Then you understand it was the testing time and now you have become so strong that nothing in the universe can stop you. Now you don't have to beg for anything. You gained the strength and with this strength you can write your second half of your story with all the colours you dreamed of. That's the power of dream. So don't give up, you are born in this world to re write history at your terms and conditions.

I agree the current time is not in your favour. But its temporary and it will change for sure.

To be frank with you, I am also going through the toughest time of my life. For many reasons, I have been tested to the core for past two and half years. Me and my wife had seen all the possible pains. But my fight is still on. I am sure time will change. Half the time is changing and working hard to change the other half. I am waiting for it. It's a fight between me and God. I never asked or begged to God to change my time or asked him to give me a small ray of happiness in our family. No I will not do it. I pray daily to the supreme power and bend my head to thank him for giving me the power to fight till now. I don't know about tomorrow but till today he had made me the strongest warrior. Two and half years of hard core training. Writing this book was my dream. Which I have started two years back due to all the issues I left in between, but now, I have decided at any cot I have to complete it. I am writing this book by sitting entire night without sleep and reducing my sleep to two to three hours. As I have other commitment in day time, which I have to dedicate time and dedicate my time to work which is my bread and butter.

I don't want to tell you now in detail. But when my time changes, I will surely write my past two and half year experience. God was kind enough to keep me alive with all body parts, mind and all sensory organs at full productive state. Today when I look back, I feel proud that without any help from others. We have faced all the tough time and more important I almost completed the book. I understand one thing in my life. When an adverse situation hit you like a comet. Then don't get panic. Just look upside and give him a smile and without any complains or grievances start the battle. Once you overcome the situation then also look up and say Thank you. It's as simple as that. As I said, life is not at all complicated. If we understand this fact, everything is so simple.

One thing again I want to tell you. Don't search for happiness everywhere in the world. Search for happiness from inside. If you get the find the source of happiness from inside, then you will be happy and joyful without any reason.

If anyone in this vast world can be benefited by this book then I would be the happiest person. Indirectly I will get one more friend, who at least remembers my name. Someone somewhere in this world will remember me even after I die. What else can I ask for.

So it's not the end of this book. It's the start to a new me. So today onwards "I kill myself for a better me".

Wish everyone a great day, year and an entire life ahead.

Always believe in yourself and share this book with your friends and family and give good rating for the book. Just kidding.

Bye and Take care.

From Truly Yours

Vijaya Kumar J

9 789358 190762

Printed at Repro India Ltd.